Contents

About the Creativity, Culture and Education (CCE) Literature Review Series 06
Foreword 09
Introduction 11

Part A – Food for thought 13

1. Why change schools 13
2. What is change? 15
   2.1. Thinking of change as both process and product 15
   2.2. Change as improvement or transformation 17
   2.3. Change as 'design' 17
3. Changing whole schools 21
   3.1. Understanding the school as an organisation 21
   3.2. School change as multilayered 23
   3.3. A caveat 25
4. Two alternative models for change 27
   4.1. Doing more to help all children learn: the equity model 27
   4.2. Educating for the 21st century: the futures model 31
   4.3. Summary 41

Part B – Stories of change 43

5. Lessons from history 43
   5.1. School effectiveness and school improvement (SESI) 43
   5.2. School and practitioner based inquiry 44
   5.3. Lessons 44
6. A framework for change 47
   6.1. The timing of, and time for, whole school change 47
   6.2. A supportive framework 50
   6.3. Summary 53
7. How do schools change, and what do changing schools do? 55
   7.1. Change processes in the school 55
   7.2. School structures to support whole school change 58
   7.3. Networks to support school change 60
   7.4. Leadership of change 62
   7.5. The importance of context 66
   7.6. Summary: how can school change be sustained and extended? 68

8. Concluding remarks 71
Appendix – International change programmes and movements 73
i) Reform programmes 73
ii) Change movements 83
iii) Summary 84
iv) Further reform programmes to investigate 85
References 87

About the Creativity, Culture and Education Literature Review Series

Creativity, Culture and Education (CCE) is a national charity with a vision for all children, regardless of their background, to experience and access the diverse range of cultural activities in England because these opportunities can enhance their aspirations, achievements and skills. We promote the value and impact of creative learning and cultural opportunities through our strong evidence base and policy analysis, stimulating debate among policy makers and opinion formers, and delivering front line, high quality programmes.

Through our research and evaluation programme, we promote a systemic approach to creative and cultural initiatives and one which builds on the excellent practice which already exists to make opportunity consistent, to ensure that all children and young people are included and to place quality at the core of any creative or cultural experience.

CCE's work includes:

- **Creative Partnerships** - England's flagship creative learning programme fosters long-term partnerships between schools and creative professionals to inspire, open minds and harness the potential of creative learning. The programme has worked with just under 1 million children, and over 90,000 teachers in more than 8,000 projects in England. www.creative-partnerships.com
- **Find Your Talent** - how we can help children and young people to access arts and culture: www.findyourtalent.org

Fostering creativity is fundamentally important because creativity brings with it the ability to question, make connections, innovate, problem solve, communicate, collaborate and to reflect critically. These are all skills demanded by contemporary employers and will be vital for young people to play their part in a rapidly changing world.

Our programmes can have maximum impact if teachers, parents, children, young people and practitioners themselves learn from the experience and activities delivered through the programmes. For this reason, one of the most significant legacies will be the product of our research and evaluation and how that is effectively communicated to stakeholders.

However, because Creativity, Culture and Education works by creating partnerships drawn from the widest fields of endeavour, the different stakeholders recognise that there is often a 'knowledge gap' between reflection, analysis, and learning. In addition, the wide focus of approach – which is fundamental to the nature of creativity – means that people are often working at the limit of their disciplines.

For these reasons we have commissioned a series of literature reviews exploring the key issues in current literature and summarising the history and latest developments in each subject. Each review is written by an experienced and respected author in their field. They aim to be accessible, clearly referenced and to act as 'stepping-stone' resources to underpin the research conducted by and for Creativity, Culture and Education.

This report surveys … the reasons why people engage in school change,… the main processes describing how such change occurs, … questions assumptions about the purpose of change as well as getting us to think about how we evaluate change and demonstrate its permanence.

Foreword

This review surveys the literature focusing on the history, theory and practice of school change. It was originally published three years ago, by the Creative Partnerships team at the Arts Council. The programme and team have since been transferred to a new organisation, Creativity, Culture and Education (CCE), and the report is now being republished in the new CCE format and circulated to new partners and participants in its programmes. In this second edition, Professor Thomson has taken the opportunity to update some of the details and references from the first edition. She has also added in new sections on the work of Robin Alexander (2008) and his consideration of the effect of different attitudes to globalisation on education, and a major mixed-method study that looked at influences of leadership on student learning (Day *et al* 2009).

Professor Thomson's review is especially relevant to the broader ambitions for Creative Partnerships because of the ways in which Creative Partnerships aims to offer new models for teaching and learning, and through partnership to broker new kinds of learning regimes for young people. In addition Creative Partnerships is interested in developing forms of education which develop creative learning for the future, and this necessarily requires us to revisit how and why schools work the ways they do. She demonstrates that anyone aiming to make a difference to the quality of teaching and learning needs to engage in debates about how schools work and how they might be changed.

This report surveys both the reasons why people engage in school change and the main processes describing how such change occurs. The report questions assumptions about the purpose of change as well as getting us to think about how we evaluate change and demonstrate its permanence.

We hope that the report will be a useful for those interested in changing schools. It offers a serious and robust review of change theory and should be of use to all of us with ambitions to effect structural and systemic change. If Creative Partnerships wants to leave a lasting impact on schools through its distinct and different vision of teaching and learning, it needs to engage with the challenges Professor Thomson lays out so clearly for us.

David Parker
Julian Sefton-Green

The review begins from the premise that English schools have been engaged in a serious and intensive school improvement programme for quite some time.

Introduction

The term *whole school change* is widely used, as if everyone agrees on its meaning. This is not the case. It is used in various ways, by different people, for diverse purposes, and has distinct appearances and effects in schools and school systems.

This review teases out some of the issues that sit beneath the term. It is not a comprehensive review of the 'evidence'[1], but a focused synthesis of material judged to be relevant to all those involved and interested in the Creative Partnerships programme and its approach. It begins from the premise that English schools have been engaged in a serious and intensive school improvement programme for quite some time. This has produced progress in many areas of pupils' learning. It has also now left some with a deep weariness about the latest 'trendy' theory of teaching and learning. However, schools in Creative Partnerships have shown a continued enthusiasm for development and it is to this engaged constellation of staff, and the creative practitioners with whom they work, that this literature review is addressed.

The review assumes an already established set of expertise and practices. Therefore, in selecting material, there was no attempt to repeat lessons which are now widely cited in official documents and used in schools. Readers will not, for example, find a detailed trawl of material readily available on the Department for Education and Skills (DfES) and National College for School Leadership (NCSL) websites. The emphasis was on bringing together a wide range of materials, methods and sources of further information, at least some of which are less widely known. In order to make the text readable, some of the references and follow-up sources are provided in footnotes.

The paper is divided into two sections:

(A) Food for thought. This canvasses a set of issues which relate to the ways in which we think, and therefore do, whole school change, and

(B) Stories of change. This explores some of the lessons leant about school change.

An Appendix points to some interesting international programmes from which we might learn.

[1] The process used to develop this review was not that used by the EPPE reviews. Rather, it is a 'mapping' of literature which seeks to develop key themes and debates (Kamler & Thomson, 2006). This approach does not provide an exhaustive set of references, but rather an indicative corpus.

It is thus important to connect the reasons for change with the 'solutions' offered, since different reasons for change lead to different sites of, and strategies for, change.

Part A - **Food for thought**
1 **Why change schools?**

All schools in England are obliged to change: they must respond to policies that mandate particular courses of action, and they are also expected to work for continued progress against standards as measured by student test results and school inspections. Creative Partnerships must assist schools to meet these requirements.

But there are good reasons for Creative Partnerships to be considering change in its broader and longer term contexts. Across the world, policymakers, teachers and education scholars express two concerns about schooling:

(1) Too many children and young people fail in school, leave early, or are bored and disengaged. Schools could do more to successfully educate all children and young people.

(2) Schools are a 19th century invention and the modifications made to their basic form are still inadequate to prepare children and young people for citizenship, family life and work in the 21st century.

But these two concerns can be interpreted in different ways.

> Whereas the economic purpose is to prepare young people for the labour market, education for citizenship is concerned with the development of independent thinkers who can intelligently question prevailing norms and values. Whereas education for economic survival is limited to those skills, beliefs, attitudes and behaviours required to function productively in society, education for critical citizenship seeks to promote the concepts, capabilities and knowledge required for testing truth claims and justifying beliefs. Whereas the goals of education for economic management are largely unquestioned and taken-for-granted, the goals of education for citizenship are matters for open enquiry. Finally, whereas the economic purpose of education is to prevent alienation, the social purpose is to promote societal well-being and social and economic justice (Codd *et al*, 2002: 64).

Different reasons for change (ends) lead to different processes (means).

It is thus important to connect the reasons for change with the 'solutions' offered, since different reasons for change lead to different sites of, and strategies for, change.

But before elaborating on the ways in which the equity and futures arguments lead to different kinds of whole school change, it is important to consider what we mean by change, and by whole school change.

"'Change' may be used to argue for more autonomy in order to allow and enhance self-management of schools or for stricter central surveillance, accreditation and evaluation, or for both; it may be used to argue for more room for market forces or for more parent participation in the governance of schools" (Altrichter, 2001:1).

2 **What is change?**

Whole school change is elusive in practice and in the literatures. In this section two aspects of change are examined: (1) change as both process and product and (2) change as incremental or transformative. The notion of 'design' is offered as a means of bringing these two things together.

2.1 Thinking of change as both process and product

Michael Fullan led the educational community to understand that change was not an event that occurred in such a way that a 'before' and 'after' could be recognised and measured: rather, he defined change as a process (Fullan,1982:41). However, more recent change scholarship, such as 'third age school improvement' (Hopkins & Reynolds, 2001), suggests that there are some key places in the school where this process can occur more or less effectively, and some key issues on which change should focus, namely:

- 'moral purpose' taken to be a particularly meaningful form of vision which invites commitment;
- 'capacity' taken to mean both the knowledge and skills of school staff; and
- school 'structure and culture' taken to mean the material time-space-resource economy of the school and the ways in which the school community conducts its everyday business[2].

It is helpful to go further than this when thinking about ends and means.

Put simply, where you end up and what you end up with (outcome) is inextricably connected with what you are trying to achieve (purpose), and the avenues you use to try to get there (process). Trying to become a democratic school through using authoritarian means, for example, is clearly going to be problematic and the outcome may be something far from the goals attempted. Purpose, process and outcome are inseparable.

But the end points of change are not all the same. All outcomes are not equal.

[2] See for example Caldwell (Caldwell & Spinks, 1988, 1992, 1998); Fullan (1993; 1999; 2001; 2005); Hargreaves (1994; 1996); Louis and Miles (1990).

> 'Change' may be used to argue for more autonomy in order to allow and enhance self-management of schools or for stricter central surveillance, accreditation and evaluation, or for both; it may be used to argue for more room for market forces or for more parent participation in the governance of schools (Altrichter, 2001: 1)

In other words, not all outcomes and processes are equally worth doing. To continue with the democratic school example - becoming democratic through democratic means is insufficient if what there is to decide on is trivial or so tightly framed as to be almost meaningless, or even immoral. One can imagine for example a criminal gang moving from an authoritarian structure to a collective one, while leaving its prime activity of crime intact. So purposes, as well as processes of change, are highly significant to outcomes.

Thus, the focus of change, the point of all of the effort, will affect what happens and who is involved. It is therefore important to clarify ideas about both outcome and process at the outset of a deliberate change project.

In general, and in contradiction to the notion of a unified school 'vision', schools find themselves juggling multiple purposes and processes. These may be in tension or contradictory.

> Headteachers were keen to argue that improving exam results is not the same as improving the quality of schooling. ... there was considerable reference to the strategic, and sometimes moral dilemmas they faced ... they talked of tensions they had experienced between the need to raise standards ... and their concern as educators to focus on the needs of all children. (West, Ainscow, & Stanford, 2006: 47-48).

In the worst case scenario, a focus on one outcome to the detriment of another could even lead to that other being impossible to achieve. It is thus critical that the ethical dimensions of the purposes of change are connected with the interwoven processes being undertaken at any one time.

2.2 Change as improvement or transformation

Change can be thought of as something small and unchallenging, or something gradual and incremental, or something quite radical and transformative. Some argue that in order for schools to meet the needs of all children, they need to be radically overhauled because it is the system of schooling which is at fault[3]. In contrast, some suggest that meeting the needs of the information age requires no more than the intelligent use of ICT in schools to enhance the current curriculum and pedagogy. Whether change is seen as improvement or as transformative depends very much on how the need for change is seen. (These options are discussed in detail in section A4.)

Depending on the magnitude of the change envisaged, the processes used have to be up to the level of the task, and issues such as time, ownership, and resistance become crucial (see section B2).

2.3 Change as 'design'

One way of dealing with the tangled knot of purposes, process and outcomes is to think about change as a process of design[4] (Thomson & Blackmore, in press). In an important article on modes of making meaning, The New London Group (1996) suggested that 'design' provides a dominant concept, language and approach appropriate to the times we live in. They suggest that:

Design is both a process and a product.
Design is a concept that does not pit means against ends, and outcomes against processes, in unfortunate and short-sighted contests. 'Design' suggests that there is a necessary relationship between all of them. Discussions about design need to consider questions of why, what and how, all at once.

[3] See examples of programmes with transformative aspirations in the Appendix
[4] Datnow *et al.*, (2002) attribute the notion of school design to the business world and usage in 1996. It was however used in 1992 by veteran US school reformer Ted Sizer so it has good educational credentials. However this paper uses the notion of design by drawing on thinking about multi-modal literacies in contemporary times (see also Cope & Kalantzis, 2000 and The Learning Journal)

Designs work with available resources and ideas.
The New London Group argued that we are surrounded by designs – these are the resources for creating re-designs. New designs do not spring from a vacuum; there is no blank canvas or 'greenfield' site on which the work of designing can occur. Every design is in reality a re-design, a hybrid[5].

School change as design offers an opportunity to consider the practices of real–life designers. They spend considerable amounts of time identifying and investigating the problems with existing circumstances in order to develop careful briefs for redesign. They weigh up very carefully the human and physical worlds in which the new design must work. They sketch out ideas, consult, sketch again, trial and test prototypes. At best, designers do not rush to introduce new ideas, but work with them for as long as it takes to get them ready for real life.

Designing schools could thus be a task which works with, from and over what we already know and suspect about schooling, learning and teaching, knowledge, leadership and management. It must also at the same time break with the status quo and offer something different. This requires careful thought and time. It cannot be rushed.

However, the notion of design may lead to the conclusion that the process of change is straightforward, perhaps even rational and linear, and can be planned for as a series of logical steps and stages. Much of the research on actual school change suggests quite the reverse: that is, school change tends to be messy, complex, has unforeseen and serendipitous effects and often lurches both forwards and backwards at the same time. Some of those interested in change as a process lean towards versions of chaos and complexity theory (e.g. Brooke-Smith, 2003; Fullan, 2005; Gunter, 1997) in order to understand the ways in which change can be steered, but must also be managed on a day-to-day basis. One management writer goes so far as to dub this 'adhocracy' (Waterman, 1993). Others suggest that school change is like rebuilding a plane in mid-air (Datnow *et al*, 2002; Thomson, 1993).

[5] This notion has two implications, that in designing, existing resources must be critically examined so that the work of reshaping and remaking does not simply reproduce an undesirable process/outcome: and that because designs are hybrids and are 'inter-textual', that is they always refer to other designs and redesigns – they will also be partially familiar. There is thus no entirely 'new' design. The idea of innovation as being something completely different and new is a hangover that dogs policymakers in their quest for interventions and models that appear unique.

Design is of course not the only potential alternative term for change. Goodlad (1994) suggests that the ambiguity surrounding the notion of change, combined with the overuse of the terms 'change' and 'reform' and their continued association with ineffective projects, should convince us to abandon these words altogether. He suggests the word *renewal* to indicate the dimensions of the task to be undertaken in contemporary schools.

This brings us to other half of the term – what do we mean by whole school, when we talk of whole school change?

It is not uncommon to hear of two 'orders' of whole school change (Cuban, 1988)**. First order change leaves the basic order of the school intact. Second order change shifts the basic school structure/culture affecting relationships, routines, assumptions and practices. This duality can be further unpacked.**

3 **Changing whole schools**

There are two important aspects to thinking about change in schools: (1) understanding the school as an organisation, and (2) understanding that change will be multilayered.

3.1 Understanding the school as an organisation

The ways in which we think about the school also impact on what counts as change. There are four major organisational metaphors which might be used to think about school change.

(1) School as a rational machine
If a school is a kind of machine then change is produced through the application of various policy 'levers' which work in a relatively straightforward cause and effect manner. Thus, if teacher professional development is seen as the way to leverage changes in classrooms, then it becomes the way in which to produce improvement in pupils' learning. Continuing Professional Development (CPD) can be designed to deliver shifts in learning, and tested to see whether this has happened. If no change occurs, then it is either because the intervention was faulty, or there was an 'implementation problem'. Much contemporary policy operates in this way, and attempts to evaluate separate programmes and their immediate effects as if they were discrete parts of a machine – rather like testing the impact of a tyre realignment on the steering of a car. If a programme to encourage creativity was introduced into a school-machine, then evaluators would look for the effects/outcomes, to find out 'what worked and why'.

(2) School as an ecological web
If a school is a holistic web, where everything is interdependent and interconnected, then a change to one part of the school will not only rely on other parts of the school to support it, but it might also have an unanticipated, positive or negative, effect on the whole. It is difficult to separate out the major influences in an ecological web, and this can make planning difficult, as well as evaluation. The best known organisation application of the ecology metaphor is that of Bronfenbrenner (1979; 1989) who theorises layers of influence which connect the school to wider contexts. If a programme to encourage creativity was introduced into a school-ecology, then the whole organisation and its contexts would need to be examined in order to understand the impact.

(3) School as a system

Thinking of a school as a system is not unlike thinking of a school as an ecology. However the difference is that systems can be tracked and patterns established. For example, if a school as a system is thought of as an instance of complexity theory, then making and tracking change is neither looking for cause and effect (machine) nor looking at the whole (ecology). Instead one would seek to find and use the ways of thinking, making meaning and acting that have effects within the organisation. One example of this is the systems-thinking approach of Senge (1990; Senge *et al*, 2000) and Argyris (1993; Argyris & Schon, 1974). If a programme to encourage creativity was introduced into a school-system, then it would be possible to identify the systems of thinking/making meaning and acting that enabled and/or prohibited change.

(4) School as a sense-making, collective intelligence

Thinking of school as a collective sense-making practice emphasises the ways in which people tell stories, enact dramas, use common language and develop implicit understandings as the basis for everyday activity (Boje, 2006; Czarniawska, 1997; Gabriel, 2000). Change is conceived as an intervention in the processes of meaning-making and understanding, which is then translated into everyday practice. Reform programmes in sense-making organisations are initiated through collaborative work on the simultaneous construction of new ways of doing things and new ways of talking about what is happening. If a programme to encourage creativity was introduced to a school as a sense-making collective, then an evaluation would show how the language, metaphor and symbolic systems of the school were changed, how dramas of change were enacted and played out, and how narratives about the school were transformed.

Of course, none of these models is entirely separate from the others. Machine metaphors of change generally acknowledge the presence of multiple factors, which affect what happens, and often attempt to control for them in evaluations. Sense-making approaches generally adopt at least some aspects of ecological and/or system models.

However, it is helpful to think about the kinds of tacit ideas that underpin approaches to change, to consider their benefits and drawbacks while also taking the opportunity to mull over alternatives.

3.2 School change as multi-layered

We can see that whole school change is a slippery idea. To make matters even more complex, we also need to note that it operates on and through various levels and layers.

Those who evaluate school change have to do more than simply opt for an examination of process and desired outcomes. They must focus on what has actually happened during a period of change and arrive at some definition of the aspects of change that they wish to measure. While many evaluations simply seek to assess the impact of a particular reform initiative on student learning and possibly staff and parent attitudes, a few opt for a more nuanced notion of the scope and sites of change.

It is not uncommon to hear of two 'orders' of whole school change (Cuban, 1988). First order change leaves the basic order of the school intact. Second order change shifts the basic school structure/culture affecting relationships, routines, assumptions and practices. This duality can be further unpacked.

Kendall *et al* (2005) developed a four stage hierarchical model of change for an evaluation of the impact of the Excellence in Cities programme. Their evaluation schedule begins with shifts in resourcing and processes, moves through the experiences of staff and pupils, and finishes with sustainable shifts in the structure and culture of the school. They describe:

- first-level impacts that change inputs (for example infrastructure, staffing and material resources, staff expertise and skills) and institutional processes (such as partnership operations, approaches to curriculum planning, and the development of strategies for providing support for all pupils)
- second-level impacts, where the first-level changes begin to make their presence felt on the key players within the main initiative institutions, to bring about change in their everyday experiences
- third-level impacts, where changes begin to have measurable impact on the outcomes for the target population(s) of schools, teachers, pupils, employers and the community

- fourth-level impacts associated with embedded change to infrastructure, systems and processes and with more widespread transference and spillover of practices and ideas to institutions outside the initiative (Kendall *et al*, 2005: 121).

This is a helpful way to begin to think about changing whole schools.

A scan of studies and evaluation reports of school change suggests that Kendall *et al's* (2005) fourth level impact can be further unpacked. While, at its most elementary, whole school change means simply change which extends beyond one cohort with children in one year group, at the fourth level this actually equates to a variety of material practices:

- Adding a new dimension to the school - alternative programmes for particular students such as vocational courses, extracurricular activities such as after school homework clubs, and a new programme of events such as regular trips, exhibitions and performances[6]. These do not change overall mainstream structures of the school although they may profoundly impact on students' attitudes and school ethos.

- Changing a section of the school, e.g. one or two departments, using new pedagogical approaches and year level activities such as new transition arrangements between primary and high schools[7]. While these changes affect a cohort of students year on year, they may or may not lead to …

- … change across the board, e.g. all staff using a new approach to assessment such as performance-based or portfolio assessment, the adoption of a new timetable arrangement, or new ways of grouping students such as de-tracking and un-setting across all subjects (see Appendix).

There are also different orders of change which can occur in classrooms, the places where teachers really make a difference to students' learning. Here, change might mean teachers adding easily imported aspects of an initiative or teachers fundamentally changing their repertoires of practice[8].

[6] See for example the small shifts effected through Day 10 (Peter Woods & O'Shannessy, 2002), alternative approaches to students designated 'at risk' (Thomson, McQuade, & Rochford, 2005; Weis & Fine, 2001), breakfast clubs (Simpson, 2001) and mentoring and study support projects (Reid, 2002; Simpson & Cieslik, 2000)
[7] See for example work on middle schooling (E. Brown & Saltman, 2005), creative classrooms (Jeffrey, 2006), service learning (Cumming, 1997), student participation (Holdsworth, 2000) and approaches to the teaching of art (Atkinson & Dash, 2005) and writing (Grainger, Gooch, & Lambirth, 2005)
[8] This is the difference between the partiality of the teachers' pedagogies described in Wilson (2003) and the major changes reported in Comber and Kamler (2005)

It is clear that whole school change can mean any or all of these things. The term is used as if everyone knows and understands it, but there is a variety of interpretations of its scope and dimensions. It is thus very important for schools to debate such issues and get some agreement about what is actually meant and intended by the term 'whole school change'.

But there is one point of agreement. It is generally agreed that moving to the fourth level - that is, change across the board in schools and/or classrooms - takes time and cannot happen without considerable support and commitment from staff and governors (Stoll & Myers, 1998)[9]. And, somewhat depressingly, research suggests that this level of change is rarely sustained (of this, more later).

Further, most formal change programmes underestimate the time needed to effect change and seek to measure effects too soon. Change programmes that are evaluated soon after their inception may fail to demonstrate the extent of change that can actually be achieved[10].

3.3 A caveat

A focus on whole schools may mean that students and teachers are seen as a somewhat undifferentiated group. But even in schools which appear to be highly successful, and 'changed', particular students may feel and be left out (Ainscow, 1999; Armstrong, 2003; Fielding, 2001a). All children and young people must be included in the horizons for change, and have the opportunity and experience to 'become somebody' (Wexler, Crichlow, Kern, & Martusewicz, 1992) in school.

This points to an important question that must be asked of all change programmes: Who is this change for? Who benefits from it, and how? (Hasci, 2002).

[9] See also the 2006 special issue of Educational Administration Quarterly 42(1) on the Educational change over time? project

[10] Perhaps the most dramatic of these examples can be seen in the longitudinal follow up studies to Headstart, the early intervention poverty programme in the USA (Ellsworth & Ames, 1998; Oden, Schweinhart, Weikart, Marcus, & Xie, 2000; Zill et al., 2003), and, also in the USA, in the early years class size reforms which are now showing effects in student performance in college (Achilles, 1999; Finn, Gerber, Achilles, & Boyd-Zaharias, 2001; P. Smith, Molnar, & Zahorik, 2005). It is important to note that class size in itself is insufficient for reform; it must be accompanied by pedagogical change.

It is not sensible to assume that everyone agrees on the rationale for school change. It is vital for schools and school systems to debate the proposed outcome and purpose of change programmes.

4 Two alternative models for change

This section outlines two approaches to change. They go back to the two reasons for change outlined in the first section of the paper – that schools fail too many children, and that schools are not fitting children for life in the 21st century (see section A1). They exemplify the idea that purposes, processes and outcomes are not easily separated.

4. 1 Doing more to help all children learn: the equity model

There is certainly abundant evidence to support policymakers' concerns about equity, access and participation. Statistics of pupil attainment show a persistent gap between children from families who struggle to make ends meet and children whose families can afford to give them every opportunity. For example, analysis of 2005 student test and exam data suggests that:

> There has been some narrowing of attainment gaps between the most and least deprived *schools*, but less narrowing of gaps between deprived and non-deprived pupils. Nevertheless, attainment levels for both deprived and non-deprived pupils have increased. (National Statistics, 2006: 2)

However, the gap is not evenly distributed:

> There is evidence of a widening of the gap between FSM[11] and non-FSM pupils within both the most and least deprived schools and a narrowing of the gap for the majority of schools with average levels of deprivation. (National Statistics, 2006: 4)

Nor is FSM the only factor that makes a difference. Race and ethnicity are important too:

> ...most ethnic groups make more progress than White British pupils with similar characteristics and levels of prior attainment. However, White & Black Caribbean, Black Caribbean, Black Other, Pakistani, Gypsy/Roma and Traveller of Irish Heritage pupils make less progress at primary school than similar White British pupils; and Traveller of Irish Heritage, Gypsy/Roma and White & Black Caribbean pupils continue to make less progress at secondary school than similar White British pupils (Department for Education and Skills (DfES), 2006: 6)

11 Free School Meals (a frequently used indicator for socio-economic disadvantage)

Race, ethnicity, poverty and gender play out in complex ways to produce under- achievement:

> Socio-economic disadvantage (poverty) and gender have stronger associations than ethnicity with overall prevalence of SEN (...) [But] Black Caribbean and Mixed White & Black Caribbean pupils are around 1.5 times more likely to be identified as having Behavioural, Emotional and Social Difficulties (BESD) than White British pupils (Lindsay, Pather, & Strand, 2006: 1).

And other factors, such as mobility and location, are also important in the production of educational advantage and disadvantage, although these too are strongly tied to family economic background[12] (Machin, Telhaj, & Wilson, 2006). However, the influence of peer groups seems to matter much less than is popularly imagined (Gibbons & Telhaj, 2006).

These kinds of 'facts'[13] about achievement have been produced in England for quite some time, and we are all familiar with them. They are based on analyses of large collections of population and attainment (output) data, which are statistically interrogated to find meaningful correlations. While such analyses are very important, since they allow 'progress' to be tracked and equity monitored, such findings need to be amplified.

4.1.1 Why does this failure occur?

How we understand the reasons for failure will lead to different solutions[14].

Concerns about equity have underpinned the reform agenda in England. The reasons offered for the (re)production of inequitable schooling rest on an analysis that schools have offered different educational experiences to different pupils, and that variation in the school-system-machine must be eliminated in order that standards across all schools can be maintained. An improvement strategy based on this analysis thus requires the development of common standards, for teaching, learning and school performance, which

[12] Webber and Butler (2005: 4) suggest that, 'other than the performance of the pupil at an earlier key stage test, the type of neighbourhood in which a pupil lives is a more reliable predictor of a pupil's GCSE performance than any other information held about that pupil'.
[13] Groucho Marx's well known axiom about statistics must be borne in mind. Numbers are no less subject to manipulation than words or images, and there is debate about how attainment is best calculated.
[14] This section takes the notion of policy as 'problem and solution posing' from Bacchi (1999).

can be monitored and measured. This is one approach to systemic change which aims to redress inequalities in educational outcomes. It is the approach that is dominant in the US.

An alternative set of explanations for failure suggests that:

(1) What the students learn is often more oriented towards the regurgitation of information for tests than the exploration of important and useful ideas and understandings, and the development of ways of learning that are key to ongoing education (e.g. Apple, 1993; Gillbourn & Youdell, 2000; Kress *et al*, 2005; Lipman, 1998; Thomson, 2002; Thrupp, 1999; Tittle, 1995; Peter Woods, Jeffrey, Troman, & Boyle, 1997). Connell (1993) dubs this the CAC – the Competitive Academic Curriculum.

(2) A 'transmission pedagogy'[15], in which a set body of knowledge is 'delivered' to children and young people, highlights what students don't know rather than what they do. The 'funds of knowledge'(Gonzales, Moll, & Amanti, 2005; Moll, Tapia, & Whitmore, 1993) that pupils bring with them from everyday life in families, communities, neighbourhoods and networks find little place in the formal curriculum.

(3) The individual and collective identities and behaviours of children and young people are undermined by a culture of competition, large classes and impersonal and alienating big schools (Kohn, 1998; Meier, 1995). The social outcomes of schooling are thus difficult to achieve.

(4) Schooling still tends to be too uniform in nature, and staff struggle to offer diverse learning to the full range of children.

When asked, many young people echo these concerns. They suggest that they are far from happy with the ways in which they are disciplined and are able to form and sustain relationships with peers and teachers. They also express concerns about much of the curriculum on offer. They argue for a schooling that is more personal and intimate as well as more tailored to their specific goals, needs and interests (e.g. Burke & Grosvenor, 2004; Smyth & Hattam, 2004; Wasley, Hampel, & Clark, 1997; B. Wilson & Corbett, 2001). They argue for schools which are more just and equitable (White, 2000). Schools, they suggest, must move away from a 'one size fits all' model, to

[15] This term is taken from the work of Freire (1972; 1974) and is commonly used to describe a strongly teacher directed curriculum and pedagogy.

cultures and structures which allow them to participate in decisions which affect them. Evidence of reforms which have involved young people do suggest that meaningful participation can have very positive benefits for those groups which statistically can be shown to be disadvantaged by their schooling (Comber, Thomson, & Wells, 2001; Fielding & Bragg, 2003; Holdsworth, Stafford, Stokes, & Tyler, 2001).

Parents too have concerns about schooling that go beyond choosing which school to send their children to, and whether to stand for school governorship (Barth, 1990; Cullingford & Morrison, 1999). The vast majority of parents value education (Connell, Ashenden, Kessler, & Dowsett, 1982), but see room for improvement in home-school communication and in the ways in which they are informed about, and involved in, their children's learning (Cuttance & Stokes, 2000; de Carvalho, 1997; Tatto *et al*, 2001). They are not simply anxious that their children learn the basics, but also want schools to attend to social learning and activities which enrich the social, aesthetic and recreational aspects of their children's lives (Dodd, 1998). In contrast, the vast majority of schools still underplay the importance of parental support to academic learning (Deforge & Abouchaar, 2003; Edwards & Warin, 1999; Finn, 1998; Makin & Spedding, 2003; Shumow & Miller, 2001), and offer tightly confined avenues for parents to contribute to their children's education[16]. However, as is the case with pupils, projects which involve parents from neighbourhoods living through hard times demonstrate that they can produce very significant gains for children's education (Bernhard *et al*, 2000; Carreon, Drake, & Barton, 2005; Coleman, 1998; Hallgarten & Edwards, 2000; McKinley & Else, 2002).

4.1.2 Possible educational solutions

There is a considerable and diverse body of research (e.g. Alexander, 1997, 2004; Bell, 1999; Bentley, 1998; Craft, 2005; Fielding, 2001b; Gewirtz, 2002; Hart, Dixon, Drummond, & McIntyre, 2004; OFSTED, 2002; Tooley, 2000; Peter Woods & Jeffrey, 1996; Young, 1998) which suggests that, in order to redress the failure of schools to educate all pupils, that change must focus on:

[16] There is a substantive body of international literature which documents problems in parent-school relations (e.g. Bernhard, Freire, Pacini-Ketchabaw, & Villa, 2000; Crozier, 2000; David, 1993; David, Edwards, Hughes, & Ribbens, 1993; Griffith & Smith, 2005; Maclure & Walker, 2000; Reay, 1998; Vincent, 2000)

- pedagogies, resources and tasks that assist students, or a greater range of students, to meet requirements;
- activities that promote social learning, motivation, and improve school ethos;
- support for teachers to invent, use and sustain a wider range of pedagogical strategies;
- activities that support respectful and reciprocal relations with pupils, families and the wider community.

These strategies cut across school conventions of grouping, testing, setting, and promoting students, and question the 'standards' approach. Followed through, this analysis logically leads to a transformative approach to whole school change (examples of which can be found in the Appendix).

4.2 Educating for the 21st century: the futures model

English educational researcher Robin Alexander has been highly critical of some visions for the twenty-first century. He has consistently argued that England has opted for an impoverished view of a curriculum fit for a globalised age.

> There are two broad senses in which the architects of a national education system can think internationally. They can view the world as an essentially competitive arena of trade and influence and use education in order to maximize national advantage – economic, scientific, technological, ideological, military – over other countries. Alternatively, they can apply a more genuinely international outlook (international rather than contra-national) acknowledging that global interdependence carries moral obligations from which no country is immune; and that education can serve to unite rather than divide.
>
> In the first category I place the kind of internationalism adopted by many of the world's advanced economies in response to globalisation(...) In such a climate the school curriculum concentrates on those subjects that are deemed to offer the greatest economic leverage, and students' attainments are not merely assessed, as they should be, but they are

> also translated into local, national and international league tables of educational performance (...) This, I think, is also the force of all the talk in Anglophone countries of 'world class schools', a 'world class curriculum', 'world class skills'(...) if 'world class' here means anything (and it is now such a cliché that it may not) it means 'world beating'. (Alexander, 2008: 123-124.)

Alexander goes on to argue that in a world where there are massive disparities in health and security, where the wealth of one country is dependent on the exploitation of people in others, and where ecological catastrophe knows no borders, policy-makers need to look beyond their own national interests. What is required, he suggests, is a futures-oriented international curriculum which places such concerns at its head/heart. As he puts it:

> (...) if we contemplate the increasing fragility, inequality and instability of our world as a whole, and believe that these are not only unacceptable in themselves but are also, as a matter of fact, contrary to the national interest (...) then education will need to espouse very different priorities: moral no less than economic, holistic rather than fragmented, and collective rather than individualistic (2008: 127).

Alexander proposes that competing future scenarios need to be laid out for debate and discussion.

The logical extension of his argument is that schools need to focus more strongly on their obligation to help young people to understand themselves as social beings who are able to act constructively, alone and together, in the public interest. Moving in this kind of direction requires a radical reconceptualisation of curriculum, and the generation of pedagogies that promote enquiry, debate and knowledge production. Rather than delivery technologies suited only for the regurgitation of predetermined 'core' outputs and teaching techniques, schooling policy might instead promote the kinds of mutual endeavour that are necessary to tackle the broad global agenda. Rather than simply addressing the perceived needs of a global market they need to work on the kinds of ecological, moral, cultural, political *and* economic issues that affect us all. This means more than understanding; it also means that young people ought also to know something about the ways in which such challenges can be collectively tackled.

Such an approach to the future would also redefine equity to include capabilities which allow all young people to leave school not only with knowledge and skills that allow than to make their way in the world, but also with hope and optimism, and with a sense of efficacy and agency. They would have acquired an ethical basis for living that allowed them to make wise use of the choices that they have (see Walker & Unterhalter, 2007), including the recognition of individual and social differences, and the importance of their 'place' in the world.

Codd and colleagues in New Zealand undertook a literature and web-based review of future-oriented programmes and projects across the world (Codd *et al*, 2002). They identified nine areas which were subject to futures-oriented activity: curriculum issues, future schools, guiding educational principles, ICT, knowledge society/economy, learning/teaching, lifelong learning, partnerships, and teacher education. After reviewing 97 projects in detail, they concluded that:

> (...) in general terms, future-focused research assumes that future guiding educational principles, curriculum, schools, learning and teaching might all be improved rather than transformed, and this would be achieved, in the main, by incremental reforms, such as by expanding the use of ICT, by creating 'lead' schools, or by increasing the capacities of teachers. (Codd *et al*, 2002)

Codd *et al* contrast this incrementalist agenda with the transformative framework developed by the UNESCO Delors Report (1996). Four 'pillars' of learning – learning *to know*; learning *to do*; learning *to live together*; and, learning *to be* – are proposed as the basis for a reconstructed curriculum and schooling. They also note the far-reaching nature of the New Basics curriculum project in Queensland, Australia[17] which posits four key questions as the major organisers for learning:

- *Life pathways and social futures:* Who am I and where am I going?
- *Multiliteracies and communications media:* How do I make sense of, and communicate with, the world?
- *Active citizenship:* What are my rights and responsibilities in communities, cultures and economies?
- *Environments and technologies:* How do I describe, analyse and shape the world around me?

[17] See http://education.qld.gov.au/corporate/newbasics, Hayes, Mills, Christie and Lingard (2005) and also the Appendix

Codd and colleagues develop the reforming/transforming difference further by distinguishing five different solutions taken to the problems explored in each of the nine overlapping areas:

> Different understandings of teaching and learning are reflected in five distinct discourses (...)The *reproduction* discourse emphasises the role of education in economic and social reproduction. The *re-schooling* discourse promotes an outcomes model of teaching and learning with an emphasis on raising standards of achievement. The *de-schooling* discourse has a strong emphasis on e-learning and local initiatives involving partnerships and networks. The *reconceptualist* discourse promotes critical pedagogy and citizenship, with an emphasis on the fundamental purposes of education within a democratic networked society. Finally, the *socio-cognitive* discourse incorporates principles derived from contemporary scientific research on learning. It acts as a metadiscourse which infuses each of the other discourses. ICT features in different ways in each of these discourses. In the reproduction discourse, it is a taken-for-granted feature of the knowledge economy, whereas in the reconceptualist discourse it is understood as a social practice, potentially beneficial but requiring critical analysis and evaluation, some of which occurs within the socio-cognitive discourse. (Codd *et al*, 2002: iv)

The next section works with these different discourses and identifies some of the present 'problems' and future 'solutions' that are at play in international policy agendas. Each can be subject to a range of interpretations and the purpose of this section is to indicate possibilities, rather than be exhaustive in its coverage. The paper then goes on to discuss the use of scenarios as a future-oriented approach to change.

4.2.1 Future-oriented imperatives for change

This section takes four interconnected arguments about the changing nature of the world, and thus of schools, and presents a brief snapshot of the case made. It then uses four of the discourses identified by Codd and colleagues – reproduction, re-schooling, de-schooling, and reconceptualisation – to show possible educational solutions.

(1) Schools, as we know them, are based on out-of-date thinking

Mass schooling developed in the Industrial Age to serve the needs of an industrial society. Tyack and Cuban (1995: Ch 4) note that schools emerged in the 19th and 20th centuries in a remarkably common form across the world. They call this organisational form a *grammar*, whose elements include: one teacher, one class; age grade promotion; and a curriculum divided into subjects through which students progress in a linear fashion. This 'grammar' treats pupils as cohorts, and assumes they will learn at much the same rate, in the same order, and in the same way. Pedagogy treats children and young people predominantly as a whole class with some additional small group work. In contrast, students' work is assessed and judged as if they were individual accomplishments.

In the 1970s, the grammar of schooling and its association with industry was seen as a major problem. Educators (e.g. Anyon, 1980; Apple, 1982; Bowles & Gintis, 1976; Willis, 1977) argued that the dominant function of schooling was to select and sort children into 'manual and mental' labour. Despite the possibility of a minority of working class children becoming upwardly mobile through the school system, the majority were positioned through vocational courses and segregated schools[18] to become factory workers. Schools accomplished this social and economic sorting by adopting a factory-like organisation[19]. Children progressed year-on-year through a kind of assembly line which produced different 'models' of educated young people for different occupations[20].

While the 1970s view is no longer fashionable, the assembly-line model of schooling it critiqued is also no longer appropriate. We now understand that children are not all the same and they learn in different ways and at different rates. They also have different interests, strengths and weaknesses which schools must recognise and cater for.

[18] In the UK these were the secondary moderns and in Australia technical high schools. Admission to both was managed via an exam at the end of primary school.

[19] The late Al Shankar, former President of the American Federation of Teachers, famously remarked that if schooling was indeed a factory then it was a most peculiar one, since a quarter of the 'products' never reached the end of the production line and another quarter were turned out 'faulty', that is they did not achieve the designated learning outcomes (see Doyle, 2004).

[20] This style of organization is known as Taylorism after F. W Taylor who founded the school of 'scientific management' (see Taylor, 1911/1947). Recent developments in modularizing curriculum, particularly in FE, are often critiqued as being Taylorist, as is the national curriculum with its various levels and outcomes (e.g. Bates, 1987; M. Brown, 1994; Wigman, 1997).

Possible educational solutions:

- *Reproduction:* The strengths and weaknesses of each pupil must be identified, individual learning plans developed and students grouped according to 'ability'. Curriculum must be 'differentiated'.
- *Re-schooling:* Clearly defined outcomes allow pupils to progress in multiple 'personalised' pathways which can be measured and progress tracked.
- *De-schooling:* Pupils use e-learning to work in extended networks on areas of interest. Community based learning also extends the opportunities for individuals and groups of pupils to tailor-make courses of study relevant and meaningful to them. Individual assessment occurs via e-portfolios.
- *Reconceptualist:* the diversity of the pupil group and its extended networks is used as the basis for the examination of broad curriculum questions which are democratically agreed. Individual and small group projects are negotiated; the emphasis is on meaningful activity and 'authentic assessment'.

(2) Schools are not educating children and young people for the new economy

Globalisation has brought sweeping changes to national economies.[21] The semi-skilled and unskilled employment that was dubbed 'working class labour' – and seen as a lesser opportunity in life – has all but disappeared from many parts of the country. In its place is a new range of jobs, all of which demand much higher levels of education (Aronowitz & Cutler, 1998; Reich, 1991; Rifkin, 1996). Those who work in manufacturing are now expected to manage high-tech machines which require both literacy and numeracy beyond 'basic skills' (Gee, Hull, & Lankshear, 1996; Kincheloe, 1999). Accompanying this slimmed-down, more skilled manufacturing sector is a burgeoning service sector where, at the bottom, work is tenuous and poorly remunerated. But even here, workers are expected to demonstrate high levels of team work, initiative and 'customer service' behaviours (Du Gay, 1996).

[21] For the ways in which globalisation can be understood in relation to education see for example Burbules and Torres (2000); Mundy (2005); and Stromquist and Monkman (2000).

There is thus a new onus on schools to ensure that children are equipped to enter this changed labour landscape. Young people face a future in which they must continually make risky decisions about which work and training options best position them to avoid long and debilitating periods of under- or unemployment (Dwyer & Wynn, 2001)[22].

Possible educational solutions:

- *Reproduction* – schools must ensure that children and young people are not simply educated for the jobs that exist now, but also for the various jobs that will be on offer during their working lives. Working with employers will ensure that they have appropriate immediate vocational skills as well as the generic competences necessary for workplaces of the future and the 'portfolio career'. This includes the capacity to innovate and exercise entrepreneurialism.
- *Re-schooling* – schools must ensure that all students achieve the highest standards in literacy and numeracy. Key outcomes in vocational competences will be developed for all students and tested.
- *De-schooling* – schools will develop e-learning strategies which allow young people to explore the changing vocational landscape and to participate in international vocational learning networks.
- *Reconceptualist* – schools will ensure that all students understand the changing nature of work and its implications. They will be encouraged to debate alternative economic arrangements and to engage in dialogue with a wide range of ideas about the future of the economy (Livingstone, 1998).

(3) We live in high-tech times and this creates new opportunities for schools

There has also been in the last two decades a rapid growth of information and communication technologies (ICTs). These have not only changed the

[22] For the ways in which globalisation can be understood in relation to education see for example Burbules and Torres (2000); Mundy (2005); and Stromquist and Monkman (2000).

way in which work is accomplished, but also dramatically altered communication between people and nations (Castells, 1996, 1997, 1998) and transformed youth and popular cultures (Buckingham, 2000; Kenway & Bullen, 2001; Sefton Green, 1998). It is not simply that schools must educate children and young people for a vastly changed labour market and a different world. Education itself can benefit from ICTs which offer new possibilities for the storage, archiving, representation, sharing and processing of information. The challenge for schools, then, is not only to educate children for the knowledge society, but also to educate in, through, with and about this new interconnected world.

The 'networked society' also offers a new organisational form for schools. Through the development of new strategic alliances which are local and global, staff and pupils can exchange ideas, undertake projects, develop joint programmes and add significantly to the learning available to all in the extended community. ICTs underpin this new form of communication and learning.

Possible educational solutions:

- *Reproduction:* ICT is a 'tool' which is incorporated into the school and curriculum to make it more efficient and effective[23]. Schools network together to share 'best practice'. Homes and schools are connected to facilitate academic learning and communication.

- *Re-schooling:* Schools are expected to demonstrate that all pupils have achieved specified skill levels in the use of ICTs, and to use ICTs across the curriculum. Schools network in order to improve their individual and collective performance and to 'build capacity' for change.

- *De-schooling:* Pupils and teachers are able to meet virtually across time and space. A vast range of community and institutional resources are available to allow pupils to design their own learning with the assistance of expert facilitators from all areas and locations. ICTs are fully utilised to support the full range of learners and pedagogies. Fully accessible community centres ensure the end of the 'digital divide'. (Papert, 1993; Spender, 1995).

23 International studies show that the majority of schools are still far from incorporating all but the most basic word processing, email, resource-based and spreadsheet approaches into the curriculum (Harrison *et al.*, 2003; Lankshear *et al.*, 1997; Mulkeen, 2003). Many children engage in higher order ICT use at home, although the patterns here are uneven and inequitable (Downes, 2002; Facer, Furlong, Furlong, & Sutherland, 2003; Lewin, Mavers, & Somekh, 2003).

- Reconceptualist: ICTs are not taken as a given: techno-determinism is rejected and the directions and uses of ICTs are debated (Burbules & Callister, 2000). School communities democratically decide what ICTs to use and how, and develop their own applications (Bromley & Apple, 1998).

(4) We live in a society which is fragmenting

A knowledge society[24] is also one in which social ties and communities are weakened (Etzioni, 1993; Putnam, 1995). As the privileged become global knowledge workers, and seek to isolate themselves in gated communities, cities polarise and the poor are increasingly isolated in specific neighbourhoods (Davis, 1992; Pacione, 1997). In these circumstances, marginalised populations need access to a range of 'full service' social services. These must not duplicate the bureaucratic and uncoordinated approaches of the past, but be sensitive to local and individual needs and differences. But there must also be social healing, and work to create linkages between different communities and neighbourhoods, so that population diversity does not become the cause of deep antagonistic social divisions and exclusion.

Possible educational solutions:

- *Reproduction:* Schools institute a strong discipline code to ensure order. Civics classes teach the importance of citizenship.
- *Re-schooling:* Integrated welfare services are offered to targeted children and young people in order that they can meet the required standards. Parenting classes are offered to those deemed to fall below required standards. Social learning outcomes are developed and measured.
- *De-schooling:* Schools become part of a network of community support services. Service learning and community involvement programmes require that young people be based in community organisations and institutions. Credentialled programmes in community service are widely available.

24 This term cannot be taken at face value. It is generally equated with knowledge in science and technology, not the humanities, arts and social sciences (Kenway, Bullen, & Robb, 2005).

- *Reconceptualist:* Pupils are encouraged to engage with their communities in active citizenship and community development project and programmes. The nature of social change is a key 'organiser' for the curriculum.

4.2.2 Scenarios for the future

An alternative to the 'problem-solution' futures approach to school change is that of scenarios. These do not carry the same weight of expectation as the 'problem-solution' formulae, since they do not begin with the premise of either social changes which require a response from schools, or broad social changes which produce changes in schools. Scenarios begin by assuming that change is inevitable but the directions and dimensions of change can be actively shaped and managed.[25]

Scenarios are based in elaborations of the present. They are not predictive. Their intention is to assist schools and policymakers to clarify their preferred futures and make plans accordingly.[26] They are perhaps best thought of as 'possibility spaces':

> Scenarios based on the modelling of trends or of clarifying visions – "trends-based" and "preference-based" scenarios – may sometimes share similar limitations as predictive approaches and so constrain "out-of-the box" thinking. (...) the "possibility-space" approach (i)s an alternative which builds scenarios through steps: determining or defining the key attribute of the scenario's subject; sketching a space using the primary attributes of change of that attribute; and identifying distinct scenarios within the defined possibility space (OECD, 2006: 14).

The value of scenarios is thus 'as a tool to think about what we do and do not want, and how probable the more or less desired choices are, in terms of on-going trends and policies' (OECD, undated). The six scenarios developed by the OECD are[27]:

25 See also Davies and Ellison (2003) on developing strategic directions.
26 This is the practice of foresight, not forecast. For further information, see the website of Foresight International, http://www.foresightinternational.com.au.
27 A summary of the six OECD scenarios can be found on: http://www.oecd.org/document/10/0,2340,en_2649_34521_2078922_1_1_1_37455,00.html. They have been reprinted by the National College for School Leadership (OECD, 2004). The OECD has also published a manual on how to build and work with scenarios (OECD, 2006).

- *reproduction* scenarios where there are efforts to keep things the same through (a) building a powerful centralised system which fosters uniformity to tight specifications and accountability measures. In scenario (b) the same bureaucratic system is plunged into crisis through massive teacher shortages.
- *re-schooling* scenarios in which (a) schools become major social centres delivering a range of health, welfare, continuing education and community services, and (b) schools become innovative community knowledge centres fostering learning communities through extensive use of ICTs, new forms of assessment and pedagogy, and all hours access.
- *de-schooling* scenarios in which (a) networks of local and global educational providers replace schools through the use of ICTs and (b) there is support for the full development of an educational market in which many new providers offer educational provisions.

The use of scenarios may help to address the feeling of 'being done to'. Research suggests that schools are not accustomed to scanning the broader cultural horizons in which they exist (Levin & Riffel, 1997), and thus staff often experience themselves at the mercy of change that others determine, rather than as active agents with the capacity to influence what happens to them. Considering the OECD scenarios, or becoming involved in developing some specific to the context, may help to resolve questions of local ownership and agency.

4.3 Summary

As these two models of school change suggest, the differences between various rationales for change presuppose very different processes. These differences suggest that redesigning schools and systems requires careful research, discussion and planning.

It is not sensible to assume that everyone agrees on the rationale for school change. It is vital for schools and school systems to debate the proposed outcome and purpose of change programmes.

The next part of the paper, which focuses on the processes of whole school change, assumes that discussion about outcomes and purpose is a continuing feature of change.

Current policymakers rarely regard history in a positive light, seeking to shift the blame for educational problems onto the mistakes of former leaders. However, there is still much to be admired in the stories of reform in England, and much to be learnt from revisiting and repatriating some of the practices and ideas that were perhaps too readily abandoned.

Part B - **Stories of change**

5 **Lessons from history**

There are two dominant and interconnected traditions of school change in England: (1) school effectiveness and school improvement, and (2) school and practitioner based action inquiry. These are dealt with briefly, since it is assumed readers are familiar with them.

5.1 School effectiveness and school improvement (SESI)

The failure of schools to educate all children equally is usually attributed to two causes: the effect of factors beyond the school's control, such as family income and educational levels, and the effect of school practices. Seminal research in the post-war period suggested that the reasons for inequitable educational outcomes could not simply be attributed to socio-economic contexts (e.g. Rutter, Mortimore, & Maugham, 1979; Teddlie & Reynolds, 2000). Schools, it was argued, could make a difference if they did 'the right things'. Researchers went on to delineate the characteristics of schools that are more successful in order to find the kinds of 'effective' processes that all schools should implement. In recent years, school effectiveness (SE) researchers in particular have emphasised the importance of the classroom as the unit of effectiveness, not the school.

School improvement (SI) researchers took the view that simply delineating characteristics of successful schools was insufficient, and what was required was research that showed the principles that underpinned the processes that were used for change. School improvement was thus to provide the 'how' to the school effectiveness 'what' (e.g. Hopkins, Ainscow, & West, 1994; Stoll & Fink, 1996). SI researchers rejected the notion of a simple top-down model of change and argued for school-based reform which was also 'bottom up'.

SESI researchers have been criticised for downplaying the impact of context and for ignoring the importance of pedagogy, curriculum and assessment (Slee, Weiner, & Tomlinson, 1998; Thrupp, 1999). These charges are refuted vigorously, and in more recent SI research in schools serving high poverty neighbourhoods, researchers have emphasised the importance of bespoke school solutions (see section 8). Both SE and SI researchers are criticised for taking the 'ends' of government policy as those which are desirable, with SE researchers in particular becoming skilled at devising methods for assessing how well schools and teachers 'measure up'.

However, schools have taken SESI work and mobilised the parts of it they find useful, but the growing consensus among SI researchers in particular is that the model has just about reached the limit of its usefulness and needs rethinking (Hopkins & Reynolds, 2001).

5.2 School and practitioner based inquiry

The post-war period also saw a strong reaction against a centrally prescribed curriculum which worked as if all pupils and schools were the same, and as if teachers were simply technicians who taught what had been designed elsewhere. Stenhouse (1975) and McDonald (MacDonald & Walker, 1976), for example, argued strenuously that school and teacher practice could only be improved if teachers were actively engaged in the investigation of problems and designing local and specific solutions.

Action inquiry was the main mode adopted to bring this 'professionalisation' agenda into being (Day, Elliott, Somekh, & Winter, 2002; J. Elliott, 1991; Winter, 1989). Based on the notion that research can produce action while it is in process, through reflection-action-evaluation cycles, it was widely taken up for a range of purposes. During the 80s it was reviled as one of the reasons for inequitable schooling outcomes (too much variety, not enough standardisation) but also taken up within the SI framing as an important aspect of 'bottom up' school change.

While SI researchers and practitioners continue to adjust their model of change, school and teacher inquiry is increasingly adopted by government initiatives as an alternative to prescriptive professional development. Critics suggest that this has led to the 'domestication' of action inquiry, removing its transformative potential.

5.3 Lessons

Both SESI and action inquiry have produced, over time, bodies of work which have much to say to contemporary school reformers. Current policymakers rarely regard history in a positive light, seeking to shift the blame for educational problems onto the mistakes of former leaders.

However, there is still much to be admired in the stories of reform in England, and much to be learnt from revisiting and repatriating some of the practices and ideas that were perhaps too readily abandoned.

The following sections draw on this history, as well as experiences and scholarship from other jurisdictions.

Thinking about the need for aligned support shifts understandings of change. Instead of change being top down or bottom up – or top down and bottom up – some suggest it is a matter of thinking about inside-outside change (Elmore, 2004; Seller & Hannay, 2000) **where the outside ensures that what it offers is aligned with what is required inside.**

6 **A framework for change**

There are many sources to draw on to assist thinking about whole school change. There are writings about organisations and organisational change, and writings about systems and practices. There is also a specific literature about educational change at both the school and systemic levels.

This section sets out some issues in relation to scope and pace, and then goes on to consider the question of external support.

6.1 The timing of, and time for, whole school change

It is now generally recognised in professional and scholarly literatures that school change is neither quick nor easy. Reforms are begun, appear to take hold, and then fade away, leaving little or no lasting benefit.

Serial reform is required in order to try to keep momentum, and to recover lost ground. Some reforms appear periodically – the push for phonics, the emphasis on vocational education – while others seem to be distinct and different – creativity might be counted as one of these, although some do see 'the cultural turn' (Buckingham & Jones, 2001) as turning 'full circle' (Vulliamy & Webb, 2006). The constant push for reform creates what has come to be popularly known as 'reform fatigue' and is associated with disillusionment (Hargreaves & Goodson, 2006), although the literatures on the history of school reform indicate that resistance to change is an ongoing phenomenon.[28]

6.1.1 Goldilocks time

Despite general agreement that 'there is no such thing as a quick fix' (Stoll & Myers, 1998), there is little agreement about what kind of timescales are important for whole school change. It seems that change must go not too fast, nor too slow, but at just the right pace in order to have any impact.

Cuban (1995) argues that multiple timescales are at work in reform. He nominates five, that of media, policy, bureaucracy, teachers and pupils.

28 Resistance can also be a source of assistance to reformers, since critiques are important sources of information for further improvement. Resistance also reduces the shortsighted zeal which can accompany change, pointing to 'common sense' issues which have been ignored (Evans, 1996; Gitlin & Margonis, 1995; Warren Little, 1996)

These work at varying speeds and, he suggests, the slow learning of pupils in particular inevitably fails to keep up with the speed of policy expectations.

Part of the problem in thinking about the time dimensions of school change may lie in a mistaken notion that achieving a particular change requires a consistent approach. Fullan (2005) for example notes that while the English literacy strategy, combined with the pressure of tests and inspections, did produce a substantive increase in students' learning, this plateaued relatively quickly because the change strategy 'ran out of steam'. A different interpretation is put forward by Lodge and Reed. They suggest that:

> There is paradoxically no time on the improvement agenda for the improvement focus that is badly needed: good contextual analysis, a reconsideration of the purposes of schools, the needs of the future and the curriculum needed to serve the emerging citizens in our schools. These lie at the heart of sustainable improvement capability. (...) And compression and disintegration result in damage to the culture of schools and to their school improvement endeavours. (Lodge & Reed, 2003: 54)

Fullan (2005; 2006; 2009; Sharratt & Fullan, 2009) argues that it is time for a change of change strategy. Something very different is now required in order to continue improvement: he stakes his reputation on a systems thinking approach which combines moral purpose, change at all levels, lateral capacity-building through networks, intelligent accountability, deep learning, dual commitment to short and long term results, cyclical re-energising and dispersed leadership. Levin (2008: 120) concurs, and notes the critical importance of four key factors: (1) the engagement and commitment of all adults in the education system regardless of their position or status, (2) effective collective processes for educators to engage in professional learning, (3) aligned, coherent and supportive system policies and practices and appropriate allocation of resources. He pays particular attention to intelligent 'knowledge management' at all levels of the system; this is more than simply using data for accountability purposes but refers equally to the ways in which knowledge about how children learn and teachers teach is accumulated and shared (Cooper, Levin, & Campbell, 2009).

While there is still much to be explored in terms of the timescales of reform, and how to find the Goldilocks 'just right' pace, there is a broad consensus that teacher time is a key to success.

6.1.2 Teacher time and change

Warren Little (1994) identifies five streams of school reform:

(1) in subject matter teaching (standards ,curriculum and pedagogy)

(2) centred on problems of equity and diversity

(3) in the nature, extent and uses of student assessment

(4) in the social organisation of schooling, and

(5) in the professionalisation of teaching.

Each of these ultimately relies on teachers.

While school-machine solutions to educational change see teachers as important, they are positioned as implementers (levers), rather than as professionals able to make wise choices about what is best for their particular class and school. Contrary to the machine metaphor (see section 4):

> Policies do not normally tell you what to do, they create circumstances in which the range of options available in deciding what to do are narrowed or changed, or particular goals or outcomes are set. A response must still be put together, constructed in context, offset against other expectations. All of this involves creative social action, not robotic activity (Ball, 1994: 19).

Whole system change which recognises teacher agency is thus faced with two options – to ensure the policy or reform is enacted as intended through accountability measures, or to garner teacher commitment to the reform in question.

In a Canadian study of teachers' motivation to implement reform, Leithwood, Steinbach and Jantzi (2002) concluded that accountability approaches by themselves were less than effective. Describing teacher commitment as a resource for change, they noted that:

> Reform governments would do well to consider what is to be lost by squandering such a resource through the heavy-handed use of control strategies and what the costs would be of finding an equally effective replacement (Leithwood *et al*, 2002: 115).

Leithwood *et al* conclude that headteachers can do much to mediate accountability measures: they have a responsibility to help teachers see the implications for teaching and learning of new reform initiatives. Their conclusion, that teacher commitment is a key to change, has widespread agreement in the research and professional communities.

Commitment is necessary but hardly sufficient. Teachers can do little if they do not have time to explore options, plan, trial and reflect (Fullan & Miles, 1992; Raywid, 1993; Stoll, Earl, & Fink, 2003), or if they are not positioned as reflective.[29] However, provision of such time can be problematic if it is in the form of one-off day release: not only are classes disrupted but the teachers themselves also have a disincentive because of the additional preparation they must do for the time they are away, and sometimes 'mopping up' afterwards. Some change programmes build in solutions to such dilemmas, for example, through timetabled team meetings in the form of permanent cover arrangements within the staffing complement (see later in this section).

The provision of teacher time generally requires additional funding, at least in the short term.

6.2 A supportive framework

Some early change literatures represented the school as capable of solving all of its problems and of being almost totally self-managing.[30] However, studies of devolution, an institutional reform which gave significant resourcing autonomy to schools, pointed to the ways in which systemic arrangements shaped what it was possible for a single school to do (Bowe, Ball, & Gold, 1992; Wohlstetter, Van Kirk, Robertson, & Mohrman, 1997; Wylie, 1997) and showed the benefits of particular kinds of external services and support. In particular, the CORS[31] study (Newmann & Associates, 1996) demonstrated that structural change was insufficient and four concentric 'circles of support' - with students' learning at the centre, then authentic instruction, school organisational capacity and external support – were required to accelerate students' learning.

[29] The reflective practitioner is an axiomatic goal in the reform literature, which draws heavily on Schon (1987; 1991)
[30] This was a major criticism of Caldwell and Spinks'(1988) self–managing school (see for example Smyth, 1993) and the same concern also surfaces in critiques of school effectiveness (e.g. Slee *et al.*, 1998)
[31] Centre on Organisation and Restructuring of Schools at the University of Wisconsin Madison.

There is now a significant body of research evidence which points to the importance for successful school change of:

- *external support for school sites*

This can take the form of a critical friend, an adviser or consultant who provides information and contacts as well as asking disconfirming questions which promote critical reflection and re-thinking.[32] Datnow *et al* (2002) call this kind of support a 'design team' since their task is to assist school re-design. Sometimes such support also takes the form of tailor-made practitioner and action research courses, conducted by partner universities, in which teams of staff are enrolled (e.g. C. McLaughlin, Black-Hawkins, Brindley, McIntyre, & Taber, 2006). However, many schools are very suspicious of external support (Anyon, 1997), and such people often have to work hard to gain trust (J. Goodman, Baron, & Myers, 2004).

Increasingly such support is also available from peers via mentoring, networks and visits to other places and sites. A recent innovation in the external support repertoire is the development of partnerships, collaborations, federations and mentoring relationships between schools, and between schools and private sector organisations. There is as yet insufficient rigorous research[33] to suggest the impact of these new arrangements, although some studies from Education Action Zones suggests a need for caution (Easen, 2000; Hallgarten & Watling, 2001; Jones & Bird, 2000).

- *alignment of support throughout the system*

Because schools do not operate in isolation, it is important for district/local authority and central agendas, structures and staff to coordinate the inputs necessary for change, while also ensuring that there are not conflicting practices or other impediments and barriers to change. Some US change programmes (see Appendix) now make district and network support a condition of involvement.

Thinking about the need for aligned support shifts understandings of change. Instead of change being top down or bottom up – or top down and bottom up – some suggest it is a matter of thinking about *inside-outside* change

[32] The provision of external support is fundamental to a number of change programmes including Improving the Quality of Education for All (IQEA), see www.iqea.com and www.partnersinschools.org. Also see for example Hall and Hord (1987) and Rust and Freidus (2001) on the role of change agents.
[33] There is, however, self reporting and evaluation which has not yet been tested by larger scale longitudinal studies.

(Elmore, 2004; Seller & Hannay, 2000) where the outside ensures that what it offers is aligned with what is required inside.

The notion of alignment points to vertical relations between the various levels of an educational system. It does not necessarily address the need for horizontal alignment, at all levels, between various initiatives. Horizontal alignment does more than alleviate internal conflicts and contradictions which arise as one school impacts on another. As Fullan (2005: 11) observes:

> You must have school and district leaders who are committed to interacting laterally with other schools and districts in order to learn from each other and to identify with the larger purpose of education reform.

However, such horizontal co-operation is not always easy in locations where there is fierce competition for enrolments. Educational markets continue to disrupt even the most well-meaning attempts at cross-school collaboration (Adnett & Davies, 2000; Gorard, Taylor, & Fitz, 2003; Whitty, Power, & Halpin, 1998).

- *a realistic time frame*

Researchers continue to provide evidence of the difficulties created for schools by tensions between reform programmes[34], as well as the adverse effects on teachers of the sheer volume of reforms introduced in a short space of time (Hargreaves, 2003; Troman & Woods, 2000)[35].

Trying to change too much too fast mitigates against the development of 'slow knowing' (Claxton, 1999), a key characteristic of sustainable organisational reform practice (Hargreaves & Fink, 2006). But the vast majority of change programmes have very short lives and overestimate the actual time it takes to embed new practices in schools. Most reforms are thus marked more by a brief burst of activity followed by a relapse into long-established ways of being and doing things[36].

[34] See for example the evaluation of Excellence in Cities (Kendall *et al.*, 2005)
[35] Chapman (2005: 144) suggests that the UK government made over 50 reform interventions into schools in a seven year period.
[36] See for example the special issue of the Educational Administration Quarterly, 2006, 42(1) as well as Tyack, Tobin and Cuban (Tyack & Cuban, 1995; Tyack & Tobin, 1994).

- *moving beyond pilots and beacons*

Getting past the short-term effects of reform initiatives requires moving beyond 'islands of innovation' (Tubin, Mioduser, Nachwais, & Forkosh-Barush, 2003) where only those students immediately involved are the major beneficiaries of the intervention.

Programmes which rely on the development of pilot, 'lighthouse' or 'beacon' programmes or schools are often touted as the evidence that a reform strategy 'works'. However, being in such an elevated position brings its own problems. Fink (2000) has produced a succinct summary of the dilemmas attached to such a change strategy. He observes that highly innovative schools often lose the very things that made them innovative if they are asked to turn their attention away from their own site concerns and focus on supporting other schools. In addition, staff from innovative schools are often highly in demand, and change built on staff coherence and stability can rapidly come unstuck if there is a significant exodus of leaders. He thus cautions against using 'leading edge' schools as a systemic approach.

Clearly, avoiding the reform 'dip' requires careful planning, management and leadership and getting issues of time and support sorted out.

6.3 Summary

Changing schools requires careful attention to the pacing of reform, as well as the provision of time for teachers to engage with changing practices. External support and an aligned framework are also necessary.

Sharing change leadership shifts the ownership to those who are intended to carry it out. It ensures that change is designed incorporating the range of perspectives that exist in the school. It helps to create a 'learning community'

(Coppieters, 2005; Silins & Mulford, 2004).

7 How do schools change – what changing schools do

There is a substantive body of change literature which attempts to delineate the processes that schools use when involved in whole school change. Some of this is based in empirical research, and some extrapolates from theories of change in other fields. There is growing recognition that a great deal more empirical work is required if we are to develop more nuanced understandings of what makes for successful change.

This section considers the question of leading change. A brief survey of some of the 'how to' literature, drawing attention to constraints, support and sustainability, is followed by some comments about the importance of context and individual school histories and positions. It begins with an outline of the dominant models of change found in the literatures.

7.1 Change processes in the school

Schools in the UK are familiar with particular process models of change: they fall into three broad, but not dissimilar types:

(1) A stages model

Stages models often draw on both research and experience in consultancy and/or direct practice. They specify the linear steps, or cycle, which schools need to go through in order to implement change. For example, Everard, Morris and Wilson (2004: 253-255) nominate a six stage process:

a. diagnosis or reconnaissance in which the decision to change is made
b. determining the future – deciding what is to happen
c. characterising the present
d. identifying the gaps between future and present so that the work to be done can be identified
e. managing the transition from present to future
f. evaluating and monitoring the change

Each stage can be further disaggregated into smaller parts. So for example, 'determining the future' requires examining core purpose, looking at the hallmarks of effective organisations, building vision, mapping the environment, and writing scenarios.

This model presupposes a linear rationality that may not be achievable.

(2) A characteristics model

Characteristics models are typically developed in research. They attempt to define the key features of effective change through empirical examination of actual schools. Table 1 is a comparison of four characteristics models of change.

IQEA/MSIP comparison (A. Harris, 2000)	**NCSL (Leithwood & Reihl, 2003)**	**NCSL (Harris and Chapman, 2002)**	**NCSL (Keys *et al*, 2003)**
	Setting direction – vision and meanings	Vision and values	Create shared vision
Devolved leadership school. Collaboration	Leadership across the	Distributed leadership	Involve staff in leadership
Focus on specific teaching and learning goals Respond to diverse students	Monitor performance, outcomes and expectations	Leading learning quality Raise achievement	Improve curriculum, learning and teaching
Teacher development and professional growth	Developing people	Investment in staff development	Time for CPD
		Relationships	
	Build social capital of students and families	Community building	Involve others in school improvement
		Improve the environment	
Summative evaluation external requirements and environment	Respond productively to		
Temporary structures. Formative evaluation and culture	Developing the organisation - structures		
			Raise standard of pupil behaviour
External agency			External support from advisors and LEA Funding

Table 1: Comparing School Improvement models of change. From Thomson (2008)

The difficulty with characteristics models is that they do not necessarily appear to translate easily into a plan of action in schools. They also lack the apparent certainty of stages models. They also presuppose that each school will mix and match the characteristics to meet their particular circumstances (see later in this section on context).

(3) A practices model

Practices models focus on the regular processes which underpin successful schools. For example, Brighouse and Woods (1999: 11) offer seven key practices, which they suggest encompass 'most aspects of school life':

- The practice of teaching and learning
- The exercise of leadership
- The practice of management and organisation
- The practice of collective review
- The creation of an environment suitable for learning
- The promotion of staff development
- The encouragement of parental and community involvement

Each of these interrelated practices has its own specific set of stages which form a cycle of activity. So, the cycle of management and organisational practice is planning, organising, providing, maintaining, monitoring, evaluating and speculating, and then back to planning. The cycle of review practice is policy, practice, monitoring evidence, speculating/evaluating and adjusting practice and policy. The implication of this model is that when a reform is proposed, say for example, the introduction of new pedagogies, then changes must be made in each of the seven practices by going through each specific cycle in an integrated manner[37].

Practices models begin to represent the school as already engaged in activity and not as beginning a reform from a standing position. However they do not encompass the requirement to juggle multiple policy initiatives which can put cycles out of kilter with each other.

[37] Speaking as a former head, this model seems more in tune with my experience than either the stages or characteristics models.

Other literatures on change emphasise different processes. Shields (2003; Shields & Edwards, 2005) and Ryan (1998; 2000; 2003; 2005) for example, who are both concerned with inclusion, ethics and equity, place emphasis on the processes of dialogue, negotiation, decision-making and governance. Others with concerns primarily for democratic schooling stress the need for structures to support full involvement of staff, students and parents (Bottery, 2000, 2004; Maxcy, 1995; Moos & Macbeath, 2004; Starratt, 2003; Philip Woods, 2005). And some stress the importance of systematic school self-inquiry: through critical reflection (MacGilchrist, Reed, & Myers, 2004; Middlewood, Parker, & Beere, 2005; Riddell, 2003), working with evidence (Earl & Katz, 2006; Leithwood, Aitken, & Jantzi, 2006), self-evaluation (Macbeath, 2000; Macbeath, Demetriou, Rudduck, & Myers, 2003; Macbeath, Jakobsen, Meuret, & Schratz, 2000; MacBeath & Sugimine, 2002), and school-based research (Anderson, Herr, & Nihlen, 1994).

7.2 School structures to support whole school change

Many who write about change urge the formation of a specific change committee of teachers. For example, the Improving the Quality of Education for All (IQEA) project, a well-known School Improvement programme, requires, after a school community agrees to join the programme, that a School Improvement Group (SIG) be formed. Staff in the SIG are to be representative of the range of teachers in the school, be at all stages of their career, levels of seniority and experience in the school. The task of the SIG is to:

> discuss, modify and plan the areas of focus arising from participating in the programme, and report the areas of focus, emergent issues and observations on the website and to the IQEA consultant team to enable ongoing evaluation to take place and to share findings with other IQEA schools. (Clarke, 2006)

IQEA suggests that the SIG be no less than four people and no more than eight[38]. They also require that the majority of staff take part in professional

[38] The notion that change must be managed by a small group is not universally agreed. See Hollins, Gunter and Thomson (Hollins, Gunter, & Thomson, 2006) and Thomson (1999a) for alternative structures which provide a 'critical mass'. There is also the issue of how a SIG is constructed – whether it is selected by the senior management from a pool of volunteers, or whether prospective members stand for democratic election. One or the other can have implications for the ways in which the change project rolls out.

development activities as well as in projects that focus on improving teaching and learning in classrooms.

There are, however, proposals that parents/carers, students, teaching assistants and community members might also be part of such a steering body. The long- running Disadvantaged Schools Programme in Australia for example (see Appendix) required that the school managing group consist of parents and teachers because this was seen as a tangible recognition of the parent-school partnership and a step towards building stronger home-school relationships (Connell, White, & Johnston, 1990).

Experiences in, and research[39] conducted into, real-life change programmes illustrate the pitfalls that such steering groups can encounter.

- The management group 'races ahead' of the rest of the school, thus subverting the change process.
- Members of the group alienate colleagues through evangelical advocacy of innovations.
- Members of the group are subject to harassment from colleagues resistant to change (Datnow, 1998).
- Reforms challenge powerful groups within the community (Lipman, 1998; Tittle, 1995).
- Reforms have unexpected effects which derail the project(s).
- Team members with different roles find themselves in conflict (Pounder, 1998).
- Teacher collaboration is tokenistic and ineffective (Westheimer, 1998).
- Maintaining good staff relations is valued over challenging peer practices (Achinstein, 2002).
- Departmental structures generate different cultures and experiences such that teachers can find it difficult to bring their views and concerns together (M. W. McLaughlin & Talbert, 2001; Warren Little, 1995).
- Teachers experience 'meeting overload' and 'reform fatigue' (Warren Little, 1996).
- Teachers are suspicious of the controlling effects of whole school approaches (Somekh, 2000).

[39] Some of these issues are drawn from my own experiences as a head, observation of schools as elected head of a principals' professional association, as well as research (1994; 1998; 1999b).

- There are difficulties for community, parent/carer and student representatives in representing their constituencies (Vincent, 1993).
- Community/parent/carer or student representatives have little real say and experience work on the change committee as token participation (de Carvalho, 1997; Matthews & Limb, 2003; Vincent, 1996).

There can also be problems in connecting such committees to other decision-making bodies, and in response, schools may decide to make such groups a part of the official decision-making structure.

7.3 Networks to support school change

One answer to the conundrum of 'islands of innovation', and the obdurate difficulties of scaling up educational reforms effected in one school, is to find ways in which leading schools can work with others without decimating their own capacities. This might be a network.

Networks have been a part of the educational reform process in many countries (e.g. Australia: Blackmore, 1999; Ladwig, Currie, & Chadbourne, 1994; and the USA: Lieberman & Grolnick, 1996; Pennell & Firestone, 1996; A. Smith & Wohlstetter, 2001). They are characterised by a loose organisational structure which allows collaboration across sites. They can be broad or narrow in focus, big or small, and permeable or closed. And networks can be more or less centralised. Some have controlling hubs with spokes of communication that extend out to the rest of the network. Others consist of 'multiple nodes of interconnected influence that follow less predictable and geometrically precise patterns' (Hargreaves & Fink, 2006: 179).

The basis of networking is the sharing of information. This can be done through regular face-to-face meetings or through regular online exchange of detailed information about what is happening across a number of sites.

Networks often rely on something to hold them together for the long run. This generally goes beyond simply sharing information. Many have a strong philosophy, a common language and narrative to 'glue' local initiatives together. An elaborated moral and intellectual purpose and philosophy is a hallmark of long-lasting networks – for example the Coalition of Essential Schools (Sizer, 1985, 1992, 1996; Wasley, 1994) and the National Writing Project (Gray, 2000; Lieberman & Wood, 2002) (see next section). In order to get beyond superficial sharing, networks also rely on trusting relationships and a willingness to confront difficult issues which can threaten the individual interests of individual schools[40].

Some networks have external national and state support staff - sometimes called 'change agents' (Rust & Freidus, 2001), 'brokers' (Wenger, 1998) or 'design teams' (Datnow *et al.*, 2002) - who not only carry stories and experiences around the programme and put people in touch with each other, but also organise networking events. Many networks also build integrated practice-theory partnerships between schools, and between universities and schools, which produce critical debate and a continued means of re-focusing, and ensure some cohesion and collective knowledge accumulation.

Veugelers and O'Hair (2006:5-7) suggest that the defining characteristics of effective networks are:

- student-centred learning environments
- reflective practitioner/action research
- empowerment of teachers/heads
- horizontal learning/peer learning
- deepening educational change theories and practices
- becoming a member of a broad yet personalised and caring community
- shared ownership and democratic leadership
- flexible structures, university-school partnerships
- examining issues of equity and diversity
- moving from conventional to authentic and democratic practices; and
- accelerating and sustaining change.

This is clearly a large agenda which requires time.

[40] For example, a study of a group of schools which have initiated a system of 'managed moves' for pupils as an alternative to permanent exclusion shows the importance of members being able to confront the issue of what to do when nobody wants to take on an additional difficult enrolment. This is only possible because of the trust built up in the network (B. Harris, Vincent, Thomson, & Toalster, 2006; Thomson, Harris, Vincent, & Toalster, 2005).

However, networks can inadvertently add to work intensification and increased bureaucratisation. They can also encounter all of the difficulties experienced by whole schools in attempting to manage change in a complex institution, but amplified over several sites (Dobers & Strannegard, 2001; Lieberman & McLaughlin, 1992). They are also no substitute for change in individual classrooms and schools, but rather, a complement to it.

And, as Ainscow and West remind us, all networks are not the same. They argue for four different types of engagement within networks: association, co-operation, collaboration and collegiality, where collegiality brings the greatest possibility for interdependence and the 'sharing of responsibility of one another's progress' (Ainscow & West, 2006: 135).

7.4 Leadership of change

The change literature features extensive discussion of the crucial role of leadership.

In recent times there has been a consensus that the notion of the heroic leader is neither realistic nor desirable[41]. In its place has been a strong emphasis on 'distributed' or 'dispersed leadership' through which a large group of staff can act together to accomplish particular change tasks or projects (Crowther, 1997; Frost & Harris, 2003; Lambert, 1998; Spillane, 2006). Students and parents/carers can also be part of a shared leadership approach within schools, although this is much less common in practice.

Sharing change leadership shifts the ownership to those who are intended to carry it out. It ensures that change is designed incorporating the range of perspectives that exist in the school. It helps to create a 'learning community' (Coppieters, 2005; Silins & Mulford, 2004). It spreads the responsibility for outcomes. It can cut through the bunkered organisation of secondary schools which prohibit collective and collegial activities. Nevertheless, studies of change in action suggest that such aims are not easy to fulfil and that genuinely collaborative cultures are hard to build[42].

Teacher leadership, a key aspect of distributed leadership, can be encouraged and supported (Durrant & Holden, 2005; Gunter, 2005; A. Harris,

[41] Scholars from diverse perspectives agree on this. See for example Allix (2000) Barnett, McCormick and Connors (2001), Day (2003), Glickman (2002), Godard (2003), Grace (1995), Gronn (2003), Gurr (1996), Hatcher (2005), and Strachan (1998).
[42] Hargreaves' (1990) seminal phrase 'contrived collegiality' sums up the obstacles.

2003). Strategies such as the allocation of part-time responsibility positions which provide time, and sometimes additional remuneration, can provide the 'legs' for change committee members who otherwise would have to spend considerable time after school on the kinds of investigative, planning and evaluative activities involved in school change. In addition, changes to timetables can provide for team planning, inquiry into practice, and analysis of school data.

However, there is a need for caution in relation to teacher leadership. An early study by Leithwood and Jantzi (1999) suggested that principal leadership had a weak effect on student engagement, while teacher leadership showed no impact. As a result of a very thorough review of the literature on teacher leadership, York-Barr and Duke (2004) concluded that while there was a great deal of work documenting the practices of teacher leadership, its characteristics and the conditions for its practice, very little was known about its effects. Thus, while teacher leadership can contribute to overall school change, unless it is very focused on changes in actual classrooms the impact may not appear as improved learning.

In order to illustrate the challenges of whole school change it is helpful to see how these things might come together in the role of the headteacher, who, despite the general rejection of the idea of a singular heroic leader, still bears ultimate responsibility for what happens in the school.

7.4.1 How do senior staff influence change?

One of the major benefits of considering the role of the school management team in change is that it highlights the possibility for staff to simply carry on working in their classrooms the way they always have.

There is in reality a limited range of things that can be done to encourage teachers to change. Supervision measures can attend to general competence and can, in positive environments, encourage staff to develop their repertoire of teaching approaches. Supervision includes inspection of lesson plans, observation of lessons, peer observation systems, performance management, and utilisation of data from such techniques to diagnose interventions. Heads cannot compel staff to innovate; they can simply ensure compliance with standards.

A recent large-scale mixed-methods study of the influences of leadership on student learning (Day *et al*, 2009) concluded that successful leaders:

- Create a collective vision: they have high expectations, work as and in a team, have drive, are always mindful of standards, take a holistic approach
- Improve conditions for teaching and learning: they work on the physical environment, enhancing security, securing the financial basis of the school and establishing strong but fair discipline processes
- Redesign organisational roles and functions: broadening participation and distributing the leadership
- Enhance teaching and learning: using approaches that are data informed, personalized and innovative
- Change and enrich the curriculum: through focusing on differentiation, relevance and outreach
- Enhance teacher quality: through CPD and succession planning
- Build relationships within the school community
- Actively establish relationships outside the school community
- Progressively build trust through these sets of activities

Day *et al* note that successful leaders are those who are able to diagnose, initiate and adapt. It is the 'layering' of combinations, they say, of 'fit for purpose' values-led strategies over time, which make a difference to pupil outcomes.

Based on these findings, it is reasonably safe to assume that senior staff can steer change using the management systems of the school – managing, for example, the ways in which the timetable and student grouping work, the kind of furniture used in classrooms, the distribution of computers and allocations of funding.

However, more effective in encouraging staff to take action are softer and more indirect measures[43] such as senior management:

[43] See for example Mulford (2003) and Southworth and Coles (2005)

- modelling new approaches
- team teaching
- leading conversations about change
- using the school communication systems to spread the word, and
- distributing relevant research articles.

And, as noted earlier, professional development is also critical, for example:

- professional development that is both school-based and out of school
- visits
- learning walks
- mentoring schemes
- action research projects and school-based research teams, and
- participation in wider networks.

A key issue for senior management concerns the way they deal with questions of democracy, equity and diversity (Blase & Anderson, 1995; Grace, 1995). This is an important issue in schools involved in the Creative Partnerships programme (Thomson & Sanders, 2009). Ryan (2003; 2005) for example argues not for distributed leadership but for anti-hierarchical schools in which the different contributions of people with different skills and perspectives are honoured. He outlines levels of potential involvement, the different roles that students, parents and teachers might take, and possible areas of participation. He suggests that questions of inclusion and diversity, again related to the populations of urban schools, are keys to successful reform.

Shields (2003) takes the view that heads must develop cultural expertise that is both intellectual and lived. She suggests that heads need to understand debates about justice and multiculturalism and to explicitly position themselves and their actions in the school in an ethico-political manner. She promotes the idea of grounded dialogue and thinking of the school as a public sphere (Shields & Edwards, 2005).

It is clear that there are no guarantees here and that ultimately staff must see the sense in mooted change and must agree with the reasons for its promotion.

It is worth noting that much of the school-community literature highlights the importance of good communication practices (Crozier & Reay, 2005; R. Elliott, 2003; Hughes & MacNaughton, 2000).

Those leading change activities have to ensure that the wider school community is well-informed prior to any innovation being begun, and then is kept fully informed. Staff meetings, displays, newsletters, websites, exhibitions and more unusual techniques such as DVDs and photo albums can be complemented by strategic press coverage and presentations to outside audiences. The latter are generally not merely a presentation to others but also an important internal mechanism for legitimating and celebrating the efforts of those involved in change.

7.5 The importance of context

This section has talked in generalities, as if all schools are the same. This is clearly not the case. Each school has a particular history, a specific population and staff, and serves a distinct community/ies and localities and student population (Thomson, 2000; Thrupp, 1999).

School improvement researchers initially proposed universal principles which were applied generically to all schools. However in recent years, they, along with others concerned with school redesign, have focused not only on what is common and patterned among schools, but what is unique to each one. This shift can be clearly seen in work recently undertaken in the UK in schools catering for children and young people whose families are struggling to make ends meet. Facing the potential criticism[44] that in recognising the power of context they are acknowledging the limitations of what schools can do (Lupton, 2003), Harris and colleagues for example say:

> Shifts in the external environment (e.g. new employment opportunities, new housing, specialist status) had positively affected the school's ability to raise attainment far more than any internal changes (e.g. new buildings, new staff, new resources) (A. Harris, James, Gunraj, Clarke, & Harris, 2006: 15)

[44] SI researchers, along with others (Baker, 2005; Cotton, Mann, Hassan, & Nickolay, 2003; Kugelmass, 2004; Lyman & Villani, 2004; Stubbs, 2003; Winkley, 2002; Wrigley, 2003), also document examples of schools in deprived areas that go against the odds.

School improvement researchers have argued for a 'fit' between individual schools and the strategies required for change (Day *et al*, 2009; Hopkins *et al*, 1994). They have developed typologies of schools which demonstrate their levels of readiness for change (e.g. Stoll and Fink's (1996) 'stuck and strolling' quadrant model; West-Burnham's (2005) readiness and capability model) and types of strategies that meet developmental needs (e.g. Harris *et al's* (2006) three types of intervention strategies for schools facing challenging circumstances). This recognition of context is, as Thrupp (2006: 113) suggests, a sign that 'differentiated school improvement' is now on the agenda[45].

Studies of change in specific schools with 'challenging contexts' trouble easy notions of 'success'. Miron and Lauria (2005), for example, focused on schools in inner cities, their educational attainment and the political identities of their students, and how these were formed in and through schooling. They showed that 'unsuccessful' inner city schools were those in which students retained strong ties and identification with their communities, whereas in 'successful' inner urban schools, students broke from their families and neighbourhoods and formed a middle class educated identity. This represents a thorny ethical issue which requires considerable debate.

The complexity of changing schools in such contexts often means changing the ways in which staff 'imagine' particular communities and the education that they need (Shields, Bishop, & Mazawi, 2005; Valencia, 1997). Deficit views of families and children leads to lowered expectations which can equate to 'dumbed down' work and slowly paced lessons, and hostile and paternalistic interactions with families.

Thinking about context also means more than a focus on the school. Policy frameworks impact differently on different schools; teachers in different contexts are variously positioned and prepared to undertake yet more reform[46]. Greater degrees of differentiated provision may well be required in order to effect whole school change. As Lupton (2004) argues, it may not just be school change strategies that need to operate with a recognition of specific differences, but also overall policy frameworks (c.f.Thomson, 2002).

[45] There are still some significant omissions from the SI context-specific approach. Critics (Thomson, in press; Thrupp & Wilmott, 2003) suggest that there is for example little on the debates that vex school heads about class size (Achilles, 1999; Blatchford, 2003) or ability grouping (Hart et al., 2004; Oakes, Wells, Jones, & Datnow, 1997), and nothing to assist them to help their staffs manage and mediate testing, league tables and the educational 'triage' demanded by 5 A*-Cs (Gillbourn & Youdell, 2000). There is nothing about how to do more with less, nor how to manage competition from a new smart 'city academy' with an impressive signature building just up the road. There is no reminder of the history of interagency projects and what might be learnt from them.

[46] See for example the recent large scale study of teachers' work, lives and effectiveness (Day *et al.*, 2006)

7.6 Summary: how can school change be sustained and extended?

The corpus of research on school change (e.g. Datnow *et al.*, 2002; Fullan, 2001; Hargreaves, 1996; Levin, 2001; Louis & Miles, 1990) suggests that long-term, relatively generalised change requires a combination of:

- local and regional autonomy
- support for teacher action and learning, at all levels
- external support which provides new financial and intellectual resources as well as critical feedback
- a philosophy to which schools can sign up
- school staff involvement in important debates about change, and
- networks within which schools can share ideas and experiences.

Schools which change generally have a stable staff, a well worked out philosophy through which reasons for change can be justified and explained, a structure/culture which supports discussion and debate, and sufficient autonomy and flexibility to engage in innovation.

They are not isolated – on the contrary, they are strongly connected with other like-minded schools. They are supported by external staff and by specific resources for change. They enjoy district and central policies and practices which are aligned with their reform goals.

Whole school change is a complex and somewhat unstable notion. There are debates about what it is, why it might be done, and how it is effected.

8 Concluding remarks

Whole school change is a complex and somewhat unstable notion. There are debates about what it is, why it might be done, and how it is effected.

However, there is widespread agreement that:

- there is no single recipe for change
- it requires action at the local level, but also support from outside, and
- it takes time, usually longer than is anticipated.

Change has been notoriously hard to sustain, and even where there have been some gains in learning outcomes, these plateau after a relatively short period of time.

This presents an ongoing challenge to schools and school systems, as well as to those who seek to support and better understand the purposes and practices of change.

Despite the rhetoric of 'best practice' it is not possible to simply transfer change programmes from one place to another. … Even if the words used to describe aims, problems, or outcomes, are the same, what exists on the ground in schools will inevitably be marked by singular characteristics in each and every instance.

Appendix 1 **International change programmes and movements**

Despite the rhetoric of 'best practice' it is not possible to simply transfer change programmes from one place to another. Particular policies, histories, people and places shape programmes in unique ways. Even if the words used to describe aims, problems, or outcomes, are the same, what exists on the ground in schools will inevitably be marked by singular characteristics in each and every instance.

But the specificity of particular programmes does not negate the importance of considering what might be learnt from looking at examples of reform practice. It is still very useful to consider principles and stories of programmes and movements which might be of use in thinking about the challenges faced by Creative Partnerships and the specifics of change in England, now.

This particular group of reforms has been selected because they share (or shared):

- an express commitment to equity and inclusion
- the view that teachers are central to school change, and
- a strong critique of dull and routinised learning which alienates many children and young people.

There are, of course, many other reform programmes that might have been chosen, but these are relatively well documented and seem to have some resonance with the transformative goals of Creative Partnerships. Further reform projects and movements, and sources of information about them, can be found at the end of this section.

i. Reform programmes

Reform programmes have:

- a formal organisational structure to which a school belongs, generally (although not always) voluntarily
- a recognisable identity and philosophy to which schools sign up
- a calendar of activities which are badged as belonging to the programme
- publications, website, newsletters, and
- a physical and virtual central location.

In the USA, many reform programmes are associated with a particular university and a body of research which provided the initial impetus for the programme's development.

Six programmes are considered, five of which are/were for whole schools and one which is geared to individual teachers.

a. The Coalition of Essential Schools – USA

The Coalition of Essential Schools (CES) developed from research funded by the Carnegie Foundation[47]. Studies suggested that the dominant high school model, in which one teacher took a number of classes for 40 minute lessons and students had a smorgasbord of choices open to them, not only reproduced historical patterns of success and failure but was also deeply frustrating for teachers who could not do what they were trained to do. Ted Sizer's (1985; 1992; 1996) emblematic teacher Horace became the signature for a reform programme which sought to:

- limit the numbers of teachers for any one student and limit the numbers of students for any one teacher
- reduce the scope of the curriculum, 'going deep not wide', and
- substitute authentic portfolio-based assessment for tests and worksheets.

The CES developed a charter of principles which has become the bedrock of the network (see http://www.essentialschools.org/pub/ces_docs/about/phil/10cps/10cps.html). Application of these principles involves schools reducing class size, basing curriculum on interdisciplinary questions, teachers having multiple roles ranging from counsellor and family liaison to management of aspects of the school, modifying timetables to accommodate independent learning and reduced quantum of subjects, and an extended school day and year.

CES began with a central organisation[48] but now has several regional centres which operate largely on a fee-for-service basis with CES schools.

47 The Carnegie Foundation generated a series of inquiries into the state of US schooling (Boyer, 1983; Powell, Farrar, & Cohen, 1985; Sizer, 1985). It is still a key player in its current incarnation, headed up by Lee Shulman.
48 This was originally based at Brown University with Ted Sizer. The shift from university based work to autonomous organisation is not uncommon. In the US it is not difficult for such new organizations to be granted charity status, rather than have to become private sector companies.

Schools that apply to become members of the CES go through a three stage process:

(1) exploring, when the school community considers the implications of CES and reaches consensus on joining
(2) planning, when schools work on how they will restructure, and
(3) membership, when the progress of the school is assessed by regional CES staff and staff from other CES schools.

In order to stay in the CES network, schools must commit to regular self-evaluation and peer review.

The CES central organisation supports the network through a website[49], regular publications, a continuing professional development programme including a very popular summer school, and ongoing research[50]. Research into the CES (e.g. Wasley, 1994; Wasley *et al*, 1997) suggests that CES schools do make considerable progress in redressing learning outcomes for students who generally do not benefit from their schooling, although this is not without difficulties of working from resistance to collaboration (Muncey & Macquillan, 1996). There is also some counter-evidence that student learning outcomes are not significantly affected[51]. Some researchers do suggest that a weakness of the programme remains in the workload expected of teachers and their competence in pedagogies which are very different from the norm in most US schools (Datnow *et al*, 2002).

The CES is a mature reform programme which has worked on questions of organisational sustainability. It remains a vital and regenerative alternative to the educational trends prevalent in the US.

b. The Big Picture - USA

Based in Providence, The Big Picture[52] is a not-for-profit company founded by educators Dennis Littky and Elliot Washor. The idea for the company originated in 1995 when the Annenberg Institute for School Reform at Brown University worked with the Rhode Island school district to design a

[49] CES on http://www.essentialschools.org/
[50] There is also an active blog on http://www.essentialblog.org
[51] See the section on CES in The Educators Guide to School Reform on http://www.aasa.org/issues_and_insights/district_organization/Reform/index.htm
[52] http://www.bigpicture.org

new student-centred school. It is funded by a number of foundations, including the Bill and Melinda Gates Foundation, and its Board of Directors includes both Ted Sizer and Deborah Meier.

The schools that The Big Picture supports are small in size so that each child can be well known by at least one adult. Schools must adhere to 10 distinguishing features which include personalisation, authentic assessment, parent/family engagement, college preparation, and learning in the real world. There are five learning principles which are infused throughout the schools: communication, empirical reasoning, personal qualities, quantitative reasoning and social reasoning.

Big Picture schools not only work on curriculum, pedagogy and assessment but also on the physical environment of schooling, often starting with community participation in the design of buildings. This aspect of their work is unique to US reform programmes.

The Big Picture now supports nearly 40 schools through a website, conferences, advisory support and professional development programmes.

c. Productive Pedagogies - Australia

The Productive Pedagogies project grew from a longitudinal study of schools in Queensland, Australia (School of Education University of Queensland, 2001). Drawing on the work of Newmann and Associates (1996) in the US and Australian traditions of reform and research, the study examined four dimensions of pedagogy: intellectual quality, connectedness, supportive classroom environment and working with and across differences. In order to maximize academic and social outcomes, all four had to be equally present at the highest levels. The study also examined school leadership and organisation, developing the notion that leadership itself operates pedagogically (Lingard, Christie, Hayes, & Mills, 2003).

Taking up the notion of productive pedagogies, the state education system then developed a radical new curriculum and assessment framework, the New Basics and Rich Tasks[53]. Together these form the basis of a reform programme which has now extended beyond Queensland into New South Wales and other states of Australia. Volunteer schools work in partnership with a university partner to convert the three-part framework into classroom practice in school settings (Hayes *et al*, 2005).

Productive Pedagogies thus:

- develops density of leadership in the school
- brings together teachers and 'critical friends' in a reform co-construction partnership
- adopts an action research model of development,[54] and
- connects networks of schools.

The development of Productive Pedagogies is supported in both Queensland and New South Wales through government funding in the form of school grants. In other states, individual schools can decide to work with the framework using their own funding.

Because the project is still relatively new it is difficult to know how it will build in sustainability. However it is already generating research (e.g. Hayes et al, 2005) and a set of materials that could form the basis of a more autonomous reform programme.

The ways in which universities and schools work together, combined with its radical approach to curriculum, pedagogy and assessment, make Productive Pedagogies worthy of serious international interest.

d. The Comer School Development Programme - USA

This reform programme is based on the work of James Comer and is physically coordinated from Yale University[55]. Comer's work centres on the need for schools to cater fully for the developmental needs of children by engaging with their families and communities in respectful and healthy partnerships. Comer argues that schools can become engines of community change as well as significantly altering the inequitable and unjust patterns of education. The programme aims to restructure the whole school through strengthening home-school relations, and educating staff in the priorities of children's social, emotional and academic development.

53 See http://education.qld.gov.au/corporate/newbasics/ and for summaries of research see http://education.qld.gov.au/corporate/newbasics/html/research/research.html
54 This is a hallmark of Australian reform initiatives – see Kemmis and McTaggart (1988) for an example
55 http://www.info.med.yale.edu/comer

Comer schools adopt a common structure:

- The School Planning and Management team develops a Comprehensive School Plan
- The Students and Staff Support Team, which includes non-teachers and other agencies, plans co-ordinated support for individuals and groups of students
- The Parent Team works on parent engagement and participation as well as community development.

The school operates according to a set of guiding principles which emphasise 'no fault', consensus and collaboration.

Schools can only opt into the Comer programme if there are a number of schools doing so in a district because the programme relies on local networks, external support and systemic co-ordination. This stipulation means that the programme becomes embedded in the everyday operations of school districts and is included in its regular staffing and financial arrangements[56]. However Yale provides a continuing source of support through conferences, research and publications[57] and a website.

Datnow *et al* (2002) suggest that an early weakness of the approach was an emphasis on social and emotional development to the detriment of teaching and learning. They note that this has now been rectified.

e. Disadvantaged Schools Programme – Australia

The Disadvantaged Schools Programme (DSP) ran between 1973 and 1996. The schools serving the poorest 15% of Australia's children received additional funding for whole school change. The premise of the programme was that schools, as they were constituted, actively disadvantaged low income populations and thus, it was the schools (not the children or their families) that must change. There was from the outset a very clear purpose for the funding and for school activity.

56 Schools in Dublin are now trialing the Comer approach

57 Much of this is commercially available – see for example The Field Guide to Comer Schools In Action (Joyner, Comer, & Ben-Avie, 2004). The website has a full list of publications – http://www.med.yale.edu/comer/about/publications.html

The DSP was well researched (e.g. Connell, Johnston, & White, 1990; Connell, White et al, 1990; Connell, White, & Johnston, 1991; Hatton, Munns, & Dent, 1995; Lingard, 1997). It generated a large amount of professional development material focused specifically on helping teachers understand the relationship between poverty and education, the importance of parent participation, and the need for pedagogical, curriculum and assessment reform, particularly literacy and numeracy (e.g. Comber, 1996; Comber, 1997; Connell, 1993; D. Goodman, 1979; Kemmis, Cole, & Suggett, 1983; McRae, 1990). The intellectual debate within the DSP brought together international and national university-based researchers, teachers and parent activists in a rich mixture whose influence went far beyond the programme (Thomson, 2007).

A condition of funding was that each school would have a specific reform committee made up of teachers and parents; this structure was mirrored at programme level with state committees having the same composition. This requirement was not simply symbolic but served to ensure that school administrations did not make decisions about significant amounts of funding without consultation.

DSP schools mostly used their additional funds for community liaison positions and release time for staff (Commonwealth Schools Commission & Disadvantaged Schools Program, 1979; Thomson & Wilkins, 1997). They piloted and made common the use of specific responsibility positions where teachers took the lead in team action inquiry and development of specific projects. These were complementary to the role of Heads of Department and thus generated leadership density in the school.

In its later years the national organisation of the DSP changed and it was no longer able to aggregate learning from schools nor to work systematically on continuing to generate new understandings and debate about reform. The DSP proved unable to withstand the national push for quantifiable measures of improvement, and was replaced by a specific programme focused on literacy.

During its lifetime and beyond, it had a profound influence on other reform programmes across the country, training a large number of parent and teacher leaders.

f. The National Writing Project – USA

The National Writing Project is a nation-wide non-profit organisation that promotes professional development in writing for primary and secondary school teachers. The NWP consists of a network of sites through which teachers in every state access courses and programmes subcontracted by the NWP to local non-profit organisations and higher education institutions. Since its inception in 1974, it has served over 2 million teachers[58]. The federal government pays 50% of the costs of courses. The remainder is raised from participants.

A popular feature of the NWP is the summer school programme. This epitomises the strong philosophy which underpins its activity. The NWP does not simply focus on teachers developing pedagogies but also encourages them to become strong, confident writers themselves, so that they can model for children the range of writing practices that are part of the language curriculum.

The central NWP organisation provides:

- specific support for local NWP site leaders
- networking between sites by means of meetings and publications
- research into NWP's scope and effectiveness
- publications from NWP sites, and
- an interactive website.[59]

The NWP brings together teacher 'experts', academics and professional writers in productive conversations. It has stimulated practitioner research into writing, the assessment of writing, and broader school reform[60]. It creates specific writing- oriented leadership within schools and school districts and thus its practices are diffused throughout the wider system (Lieberman & Wood, 2002). School-based leaders also promote NWP activities helping to create a sustainable organisation.

[58] Data from government website - http://www.ed.gov/programs/writing/index.html
[59] See http://www.writingproject.org
[60] See http://www.writingproject.org/Publications/books/

g. The Israel experiment programme

The Israel experiment programme is funded through the Division for Experiments and Innovations (DEI)[61]. It provides funding to schools for five years to develop 'models' of reform. These models are to be adapted by other schools, and thus each reform initiative must demonstrate a sound theoretical basis and method of development, and have an explicit school-based infrastructure.

One of the requirements of funding is that schools nominate a specific teacher as a documenter of the innovation. This teacher has time release and the DEI provides specific training in school-based research and evaluation (Bar-Niv Niv, 2006).

The first year in the five year funding cycle is for planning and preparation, the second to fourth years are implementation of the innovation, while in the fifth and final year schools are expected to produce formal documentation in the form of a book. This book is published and distributed to all schools in the system.

The DEI supports innovations through:

- the creation of networks
- team based training of school-based innovation leaders , and
- preparation of schools for the introduction of change.

Schools which are deemed to be 'outstanding' then become training centres, which support other schools in the programme. At present there are 10 training centres and 150 schools involved in the Experiment programme.

h. The A+ Schools Reform

The A+ Schools reform movement began in North Carolina in 1995 working in 25 schools. It has now extended to Arkansas and Oklahoma and during its life it has received almost US$1 million from the Thomas S. Kenan Institute

[61] This information from an rtf document The Division of Experiments and Innovations (DEI) on http://cms.education.gov.il/NR/rdonlyres/AB10F782-73EE-4746-9EB9-766F15BAF336/2184/Innovative_Schools.rtf Accessed 7 June 2006

for the Arts and the Ford Foundation. The reforms involve funding schools to increase arts instruction and arts integration through involving creative artists, a network organization, and an approach which asks schools to think creatively, rather than required them to meet mandated reforms. This produces, say evaluators, strong school level buy-in and adaptation to local needs (Adkins & Gunzenhauser, 2005; Gordon & Patterson, 2008; Noblit, Dickson, Wilson, & McKinney, 2009).

Schools involved with the A+ programme placed arts at the centre of the curriculum and made five core commitments:

(1) Students should have increased exposure to arts instruction. This commitment required all pilot schools to have full-time staff in four arts forms (music, visual art, dance, drama) with one full hour of arts instruction per day and exposure to all four arts forms each week. However not all schools managed to achieve this because of problems with state funding.

(2) Schools should foster two –way arts integration. By two-way the A+ reforms envisaged a complementary relationship between arts and the core curriculum with the core curriculum being infused with arts and vice versa. Evaluations suggest that this meant that in addition to the arts not being relegated to a minor curriculum place, students actually encountered mainstream curriculum more often.

(3) Teachers should tap students' multiple intelligences. Professional development focused on philosophical grounding as well as practical strategies.

(4) Schools should adopt an integrated, thematic approach to major ideas in the curriculum, This not only afforded the opportunity to connect the arts to other areas of instruction, but also allowed students to show what they had learnt in creative ways.

(5) Schools should strengthen their relationships with parents and the community. Schools were encouraged to draw on family and community resources in order to extend students' cultural and artistic experiences.

These commitments are supported by an organization which offers intensive five day summer institutes for schools, designated A+ fellows in schools who offer leadership both within their schools and across the network, and best practices conferences.

See http://handbook.laartsed.org/modles.index.ashx?md=4

ii. Change movements

Change movements differ from programmes in that they have no formal structure. They become a movement because there is a body of theory and practice, usually generated from multiple sources. There are generally specific champions (people, institutions or organisations) whose work is foundational. The key ideas underpin development in a number of sites and jurisdictions which proceed independently, but are often connected in loose communication networks.

Two examples are:

a. The middle schooling movement

Middle schools are not to be confused with junior high schools. Middle schooling has a basis in a body of scholarship about the specific educational needs of young adolescents and begins from a critique of the inadequacies of conventional high schools (e.g. Barratt, 1997; Beane, 1997; E. Brown & Saltman, 2005; Carrington, 2006; Dickinson, 2001; Strahan, Cooper, & Ward, 2001).

Those interested in middle schooling undertake reforms which are structural/cultural and academic. There is typically a reduced number of teachers for students, a multidisciplinary and thematic curriculum organised around key questions of significance, and the use of home rooms and teaching teams.

Middle schools have been created in a number of locations and there are some middle school professional associations that provide networking and some support for their leaders, teachers and parents[62]. Middle schooling has powerful intellectual backing and continues to generate research and professional writing.

62 See for example http://www.middleweb.com/

b. Small schools – human scale education

Small school or human scale education[63] is a reform movement which has been taken up by individual schools through networking, and by some school districts, particularly in rural areas. It begins with a critique of the impersonal nature of large schools and argues that the pedagogical relationship relies on everybody knowing each other. It is suggested that small schools are particularly important for children who, by virtue of their class, race or ethnicity, are most likely to do less well in school. This philosophy has encouraged large schools to think about how to break themselves into smaller sub-schools and schools-within-schools.

The small school movement has powerful backers in the United States where research suggests that size does matter (e.g. Howley, 2003).

iii. Summary

A brief examination of some reform programmes and movements suggests that they share some common features:

- A strong central philosophy which encourages schools to go beyond the 'standard model' of education
- Professional development for teachers
- Networking between sites and practitioners
- A central focus on teaching and learning with associated changes to school structures and cultures
- External support and a co-construction of change – reform is a joint accomplishment (Datnow et al, 2002: 141)

Strong programmes also tend to have a central organisation which provides coordination, research and publications.

This tells us something about what must happen inside and outside schools in order for change to 'stick'. It suggests that there is some reassurance in numbers, as well as considerable gains in learning which are greater than any single school might achieve. It also highlights the contribution that

63 See in the USA http://www.smallschoolsproject.org/ and in the UK http://www.smallschools.org.uk/ and http://www.hse.org.uk/

reform programmes and projects can make to the wider system, not through the provision of exemplary stories, but rather through the building of a group of experienced reform leaders.

iv. Further reform programmes to investigate

The USA has spawned a significant number of school reform programmes, in part because of the availability of funding from large foundations and its capacity to provide not-for-profit legal status.

There are online a series of compendia of reform projects:

See:
http://dmoz.org/Society/Issues/Education/Education_Reform/
and
http://www.nwrel.org/spcd/catalog/modellist.asp

There is also an evaluative list: *The Educators Guide to School Reform* on **http://www.aasa.org/issues_and_insights/district_organization/Reform/index.htm**
This contains summaries of reform programmes and evaluations from research evidence of their impact on students' learning.

Another evaluation of reforms available online is
Wang, M. C., Haertel, G. D., and Walberg, H. J. 1998a. *Achieving student success: A handbook of widely implemented research-based educational reform models.* **http://www.temple.edu/LSS/whatsnew.htm#handbook.**

The Annenberg Institute for School Reform at Brown University maintains oversight of promising programmes
http://www.annenberginstitute.org/
It also has available a set of online tools for whole school reform
http://www.annenberginstitute.org/tools/index.php

References

Achilles, C. (1999). *Let's put kids first, finally.* Thousand Oaks: Corwin Press.

Achinstein, B. (2002). *Community, diversity and conflict among school teachers: the ties that blind.* New York: Teachers College Press.

Adkins, A., & Gunzenhauser, M. (2004). 'West Hollow School and the North Carolina A+Schools program: Integrating the arts, creating a local agenda for reform'. In W. Pink & G. Noblit (eds.), *Cultural matters: Lessons learned from several successful school reform strategies.* Cresskill, NJ: Hampton Press.

Adnett, N., & Davies, P. (2000). 'Competition and curriculum diversity in local schooling markets: theory and evidence'. *Journal of Education Policy,* 15(2), 157-167.

Ainscow, M. (1999). *Understanding the development of inclusive schools.* London: Falmer.

Ainscow, M., & West, M. (2006). 'Drawing out the lessons: leadership and collaboration'. In M. Ainscow & M. West (Eds.), *Improving urban schools: Leadership and collaboration* (pp. 130-144). Buckingham: Open University Press.

Alexander, R. (1997). *Policy and practice in primary education. Local initiative, national agenda.* London: Routledge.

Alexander, R. (2004). 'Still no pedagogy? Principle, pragmatism and compliance in primary education'. *Cambridge Journal of Education,* 34(1), 7-33.

Alexander, R. (2008). *Essays on pedagogy.* London: Routledge.

Allix, N. (2000). 'Transformational leadership. Democratic or despotic?' *Educational Management Administration and Leadership,* 28(1), 7-20.

Altrichter, H. (2001). 'Introduction'. In H. Altrichter & J. Elliott (Eds.), *Images of educational change* (pp. 1-10). Buckingham: Open University Press.

Anderson, G., Herr, K., & Nihlen, A. S. (1994). *Studying your own school. An educator's guide to qualitative practitioner research.* Thousand Oaks, CA: Corwin Press.

Anyon, J. (1980). 'Social class and the hidden curriculum of work'. *Journal of Education*, 162(1), 67-92.

Anyon, J. (1997). *Ghetto schooling. A political economy of urban educational reform.* New York, London: Teachers College Press.

Apple, M. (1982). *Cultural and economic reproduction in education: Essays on Class, Ideology and the State.* London: Routledge & Kegan Paul.

Apple, M. (1993). *Official knowledge: democratic curriculum in a conservative age.* New York: Routledge.

Argyris, C. (1992). *On organisational learning.* Cambridge, MA: Blackwell.

Argyris, C., & Schon, D. (1974). *Theory in practice. Increasing professional effectiveness.* San Francisco: Jossey Bass.

Armstrong, F. (2003). *Spaced out: Policy, difference and the challenge of inclusive education.* Dordrecht: Kluwer Academic Publishers.

Aronowitz, S., & Cutler, J. (Eds.). (1998). *Post-work. The wages of cybernation.* New York & London: Routledge.

Atkinson, D., & Dash, P. (Eds.). (2005). *Social and critical practices in art education.* Stoke on Trent: Trentham.

Bacchi, C. L. (1999). *Women, policy and politics. The construction of policy problems.* London, Thousand Oaks, New Delhi: Sage.

Baker, B. (2005). *Transforming schools. Illusion or reality.* Stoke on Trent: Trentham.

Ball, S. (1994). *Education reform: a critical and poststructural approach.* Buckingham: Open University Press.

Barnett, K., McCormick, J., & Conners, R. (2001). 'Transformational leadership in schools. Panacea, placebo or problem?' *Journal of Educational Administration*, 39(1), 24-46.

Bar-Niv Niv, H. (2006). *Interactive, multi-dimensional documentation in an experimental school in Israel: The case study of Ort Ma'alot.* Unpublished Education PhD: University of Sussex.

Barratt, R. (1997). *Principles of middle schooling.* Canberra: Australian Curriculum Studies Association.

Barth, R. (1990). *Improving schools from within. Teachers, parents, and principals can make the difference.* San Francisco: Jossey Bass.

Bates, R. (1987). 'Corporate culture, schooling, and educational administration'. *Educational Administration Quarterly*, 23(4), 79-115.

Beane, J. (1997). *Curriculum integration. Designing the core of democratic education.* New York: Teachers College Press.

Bell, L. (1999). 'Primary schools and the nature of the education market place'. In T. Bush, L. Bell, R. Bolam, R. Glatter & P. Ribbins (Eds.), *Educational management. Redefining theory, policy and practice* (pp. 59-73). London: Paul Chapman Publishing.

Bentley, T. (1998). *Learning beyond the classroom. Education for a changing world.* London, New York: Demos, Routledge.

Berliner, D. (2006). 'Our impoverished view of educational research'. *Teachers College Record*, 108(6), 949-995.

Bernhard, J., Freire, M., Pacini-Ketchabaw, V., & Villa, V. (1998). 'A Latin-American parents' group participates in their children's schooling; parent involvement reconsidered'. *Canadian Ethnic Studies*, 30(3), 77-98.

Blackmore, J. (1999). *Framing the issues for educational redesign: Learning networks and professional activism* (Vol. ACEA Monograph 25). Hawthorn: Australian Council for Educational Administration.

Blase, J., & Anderson, G. (1995). *The micropolitics of educational leadership.* New York: Teachers College Press.

Blatchford, P. (2003). *The class size debate. Is small better?* Buckingham: Open University Press.

Boje, D. (2007). *Storytelling organisation.* London: Sage.

Bottery, M. (2000). *Education, policy and ethics.* London & New York: Continuum.

Bottery, M. (2004). *The challenges of educational leadership.* London: Paul Chapman.

Bowe, R., Ball, S., & Gold, A. (1992). *Reforming education and changing schools: case studies in policy sociology.* London: Routledge.

Bowles, S., & Gintis, H. (1976). *Schooling in capitalist America.* New York: Basic Books.

Boyer, E. (1983). *High school. A report on secondary education in America.* New York: The Carnegie Foundation for the Advancement of Teaching, Harper and Row.

Brighouse, T., & Woods, D. (1999). *How to improve your school.* London: Routledge.

Bromley, H., & Apple, M. (Eds.). (1998). *Education/technology/power: Educational computing as a social practice.* Albany, NY: State University of New York Press.

Bronfenbrenner, U. (1979). *The ecology of human development.* Cambridge, MA: Harvard University Press.

Bronfenbrenner, U. (1989). 'Ecological systems theory'. In R. Vasta (Ed.), *Annals of child development Volume 6: Six theories of child development: Revised formulations and current issues* (pp. 187-251). Greenwich, CT: JAI.

Brooke-Smith, R. (2003). *Leading learners, leading schools.* London: RoutledgeFalmer.

Brown, E., & Saltman, K. (Eds.). (2005). *The critical middle school reader.* New York: Routledge.

Brown, M. (1994). 'Competency-based training: Skill formation for the workplace or classroom Taylorism?' In J. Kenway (ed.), *Economising education: The post-Fordist directions.* Geelong: Deakin University Press.

Buckingham, D. (2000). *After the death of childhood. Growing up the age of electronic media.* Cambridge, Oxford & Malden, MA: Polity Press.

Buckingham, D., & Jones, K. (2001). 'New Labour's cultural turn: some tensions in contemporary educational and cultural policy'. *Journal of Education Policy,* 16(1), 1-14.

Burbules, N., & Callister, T. (2000). *Watch IT: The risky promises and promising risks of new information technologies in education.* Boulder, Co: Westview Press.

Burbules, N., & Torres, C. (Eds.). (2000). *Globalisation and education. Critical perspectives.* New York & London: Routledge.

Burke, C., & Grosvenor, I. (2004). *The school I'd like.* London: RoutledgeFalmer.

Caldwell, B., & Spinks, J. (1988). *The self managing school.* London: Falmer Press.

Caldwell, B., & Spinks, J. (1992). *Leading the self managing school.* London: Falmer Press.

Caldwell, B., & Spinks, J. (1998). *Beyond the self managing school. Student outcomes and the reform of education.* London, Philadelphia: Falmer Press.

Carreon, G. P., Drake, C., & Barton, A. C. (2005). 'The importance of presence: Immigrant parents' school engagement experiences.' *American Educational Research Journal,* 42(3), 465-498.

Carrington, V. (2006). *Rethinking middle years. Early adolescents, schooling and digital culture.* Sydney: Allen and Unwin.

Castells, M. (1996). *The information age: Economy, society and culture: The rise of the network society.* Oxford: Blackwell.

Castells, M. (1997). *The information age: Economy, society and culture. The power of identity.* Oxford: Blackwell.

Castells, M. (1998). *The information age: Economy, society and culture. End of the millenium.* Oxford: Blackwell.

Chapman, C. (2005). *Improving schools through external intervention.* London: Continuum.

Clarke, P. (2006). *Practical arrangements for schools considering starting work with the IQEA programme (brochure).* Todmorden, Lancashire: IQEA.

Claxton, G. (1999). *Hare brain, tortoise mind. Why intelligence increases when you think less.* Hopewell, NJ: Ecco Press.

Codd, J., Brown, M., Clark, J., McPherson, J., O'Neill, H., O'Neill, J., Waitere-Ang, H., Zepke, N. (2002). *Review of future-focused research on teaching and learning. Report to the Ministry of Education.* Auckland: Ministry of Education, New Zealand.

Coleman, P. (1998). *Parent, student and teacher collaboration. The power of three.* London: Paul Chapman Publishing.

Comber, B. (1996). *The discursive construction of literacy in a disadvantaged school.* James Cook University [unpublished Ph D thesis], Adelaide.

Comber, B. (1997). 'Literacy, poverty and schooling: working against deficit equations.' *English in Australia,* 119-120, 22-34.

Comber, B., & Kamler, B. (2005). *Turnaround pedagogies.* Sydney: Primary English Teachers Association.

Comber, B., Thomson, P., & Wells, M. (2001). 'Critical literacy finds a "place": Writing and social action in a low income Australian grade 2/3 classroom.' *Elementary School Journal,* 101(4), 451-464.

Commonwealth Schools Commission, & Disadvantaged Schools Program. (1979). *Doing something about it. Volumes 1 & 2.* Canberra: Commonwealth Schools Commission.

Connell, R. (1993). *Schools and social justice.* Canada: Our Schools/Ourselves Foundation. Pluto Press.

Connell, R., Ashenden, D., Kessler, S., & Dowsett, G. (1982). *Making the difference. Schools, families and social divisions.* Sydney: Allen & Unwin.

Connell, R. W., Johnston, K., & White, V. (1990). *Measuring up. Assessment of student outcomes and evaluation of program effectiveness and the educational implications for child poverty in the Disadvantaged Schools Program.* Canberra: Schools Council, National Board of Employment, Education and Training.

Connell, R. W., White, V., & Johnston, K. (1990). *Poverty, education and the Disadvantaged Schools Program (DSP). Project overview and discussion of policy questions.* Sydney: Poverty, Education and the DSP Project, Macquarie University.

Connell, R. W., White, V., & Johnston, K. (1991). *Running twice as hard: The Disadvantaged Schools Program in Australia.* Geelong, Victoria: Deakin University Press.

Cooper, A., Levin, B., & Campbell, C. (2009). 'The growing (but still limited) importance of evidence in education policy and practice'. *Journal of Educational Change*, 10(2-3), 159-171.

Cope, B., & Kalantzis, M. (Eds.). (2000). *Multiliteracies. Literacy learning and the design of social futures.* Melbourne: Macmillan.

Coppieters, P. (2005). 'Turning schools into learning organisations.' *European Journal of Teacher Education,* 28(2), 129-139.

Cotton, T., Mann, J., Hassan, A., & Nickolay, S. (2003). *Improving primary schools, improving communities.* Stoke on Trent: Trentham.

Craft, A. (2005). *Creativity in schools: tensions and dilemmas.* London: Routledge.

Crowther, F. (1997). 'Teacher leadership: explorations in theory and practice'. *Leading and Managing,* 2(4), 304 - 321.

Crozier, G. (2000). *Parents and schools. Partners or protagonists?* Stoke on Trent, UK: Trentham Books.

Crozier, G., & Reay, D. (Eds.). (2005). *Activating participation. Parents and teachers working towards partnerships.* Stoke on Trent: Trentham.

Cuban, L. (1988). *The managerial imperative and the practice of leadership in schools.* New York: State University of New York Press.

Cuban, L. (1995). 'The myth of failed school reform.' *Education Week, November 1* (**http://www.edweek.com.** Accessed 26 April, 2010).

Cullingford, C., & Morrison, M. (1999). 'Relationships between parents and schools: a case study.' *Educational Review*, 51(3), 253-262.

Cumming, J. (1997). *Community based learning. Adding value to programs involving service Agencies and Schools.* Sydney: Dusseldorp Skills Forum.

Cuttance, P., & Stokes, S. (2000). *Reporting on student and school achievement.* Canberra: Commonwealth Department of Education, Training and Youth Affairs.

Czarniawska, B. (1997). *Narrating the organisation. Dramas of institutional identity.* Chicago: University of Chicago Press.

Datnow, A. (1998). *The gender politics of educational change.* Washington DC: Falmer Press.

Datnow, A., Hubbard, L., & Mehan, H. (2002). *Extending educational reform: From one school to many.* London: RoutledgeFalmer.

David, M. (1993). *Parents, gender and education reform.* Cambridge: Polity Press.

David, M., Edwards, R., Hughes, M., & Ribbens, J. (1993). *Mothers and education: Inside out? Exploring family-education policy and experience.* New York: St Martins Press.

Davies, B., & Ellison, L. (2003). *The new strategic direction and development of the school.* London: Routledge.

Davis, M. (1992). *City of quartz. Excavating the future in Los Angeles.* London: Vintage.

Day, C. (2003). 'What successful leadership in schools looks like: implications for policy and practice.' In B. Davies & J. West-Burnham (Eds.), *Handbook of educational leadership and management* (pp. 187-204). London: Pearson, Longman.

Day, C., Elliott, J., Somekh, B., & Winter, R. (2002). *Theory and practice in action research.* Oxford: Symposium Books.

Day, C., Sammons, P., Hopkins, D., Harris, A., Leithwood, K., Gu, Q., *et al* (2009). *The impact of school leadership on pupil outcomes, DCSF Research Report -RR108.* London: Department for Children, Schools and Families.

Day, C., *et al* (2006). *Variations in teachers' work, lives and effectiveness. Research report 743.* London: Department for Education and Skills (DfES).

de Carvalho, M. (2001). *Rethinking family-school relations: A critique of parental involvement in schooling.* Mahwah, NJ: Lawrence Erlbaum.

Delors, J. (1996). *Learning. The treasure within: Report to UNESCO of the International Commission on Education for the Twenty-First Century.* Paris: UNESCO.

Department for Education and Skills (DfES). (2005). *Ethnicity and education: the evidence on minority ethnic pupils aged 5–16:* Department for Education and Skills. **http://publications.teachernet.gov.uk/default.aspx?PageFunction=productdetails&PageMode=publications&ProductId=DFES-0208-2006&.** Accessed 26 April, 2010.

Desforges, C., & Abouchaar, A. (2003). *The impact of parental involvement, parental support and family education on pupil achievement and adjustment, A literature review.* DfES Research Report 433. Norwich: The Queen's Printer.

Dickinson, T. (Ed.). (2001). *Reinventing the middle school.* New York: Routledge.

Dobers, P., & Strannegard, L. (2001). 'Lovable networks - a story of affection, attraction and treachery.' *Journal of Organisational Change Management,* 14(1), 28-49.

Dodd, A. (1998). 'What can educators learn from parents who oppose curricular and classroom practices?' *Journal of Curriculum Studies, 30*(4), 461-477.

Downes, T. (2002). 'Children's and families' use of computers in Australian homes'. *Contemporary Issues in Early Childhood,* 3(2), 182-196.

Doyle, D. (2004). 'The knowledge guild'. *Education Next,* **http://educationnext.org/theknowledgeguild/.** Accessed 26 April, 2010

Du Gay, P. (1996). *Consumption and identity at work.* London: Sage.

Durrant, J., & Holden, G. (2005). *Teachers leading change.* London: Paul Chapman.

Dwyer, P., & Wynn, J. (2001). *Youth, education and risk. Facing the future.* London: RoutledgeFalmer.

Earl, L., & Katz, S. (2006). *Leading schools in a data-rich world. Harnessing data for school improvement.* Thousand Oaks: Corwin Press.

Easen, P. (2000). 'Education Action Zones: Partnership is no panacea for progress'. *Westminster Studies in Education,* 23, 255-269.

Edwards, A., & Warin, J. (1999). 'Parental involvement in raising the achievement of primary school pupils: Why bother?' *Oxford Review of Education,* 25(3), 325-341.

Eirenreich, B. (2001). *Nickeled and dimed. On (not) getting by in America.* New York: Henry Holt.

Eirenreich, B. (2005). *Bait and switch. The futile pursuit of the American dream.* New York: Henry Holt.

Elliott, J. (1991). *Action research for educational change.* Milton Keynes: Open University Press.

Elliott, R. (2003). 'Sharing care and education: parents' perspectives'. *Australian Journal of Early Childhood Education,* 28(4), 14-21.

Ellsworth, J., & Ames, L. (Eds.). (1998). *Critical perspectives on Project Head Start. Revisioning hope and challenge.* Albany, New York: State University of New York Press.

Elmore, R. (2004). *School reform from the inside-out.* Cambridge, MA: Harvard University Press.

Etzioni, A. (1993). *The spirit of community. The reinvention of American society.* New York: Touchstone.

Evans, R. (1996). *The human side of school change: reform, resistance and the real life problems of innovation.* San Francisco: Jossey Bass.

Everard, K. B., Morris, G., & Wilson, I. (2004). *Effective school management* (4th ed.). London: Sage.

Facer, K., Furlong, J., Furlong, R., & Sutherland, R. (2003). *Screen play. Children and computing in the home.* London: RoutledgeFalmer.

Fielding, M. (2001a). 'Students as radical agents of change'. *Journal of Educational Change,* 2(2), 123-141.

Fielding, M. (Ed.). (2001b). *Taking education really seriously. Four years hard labour.* London & New York: RoutledgeFalmer.

Fielding, M., & Bragg, S. (2003). *Students as researchers; making a difference.* Cambridge: Pearson.

Fine, M., & Weis, L. (1998). *The unknown city. The lives of poor and working class young adults.* Boston: Beacon Press.

Fink, D. (2000). 'The attrition of educational change over time: The case of 'innovative', 'model', 'lighthouse' schools'. In N. Bascia & A. Hargreaves (eds.), *The sharp edge of educational change. Teaching, leading and the realities of reform* (pp. 29-51). London: RoutledgeFalmer.

Finn, J. (1998). 'Parental engagement that makes a difference'. *Educational Leadership, 55*(8), 20-24.

Finn, J., Gerber, S., Achilles, C., & Boyd-Zaharias, J. (2001). 'The enduring effects of small classes'. *Teachers College Record 103 (2)* pp 145 - 183

Freire, P. (1972). *Pedagogy of the oppressed.* Great Britain: Penguin.

Freire, P. (1974). *Education: the practice of freedom.* London: Writers and Readers Publishing Cooperative.

Frost, D., & Harris, A. (2003). 'Teacher leadership: towards a research agenda'. *Cambridge Journal of Education, 33,* 479-498.

Fullan, M. (1982). *The meaning of educational change.* New York: Teachers College Press.

Fullan, M. (1993). *Change forces. Probing the depths of educational reform.* London: Falmer.

Fullan, M. (1999). *Change forces. The sequel.* London: Falmer.

Fullan, M. (2001). *Leading in a culture of change.* San Francisco: Jossey-Bass.

Fullan, M. (2005). *Leadership and sustainabilty: System thinkers in action.* Thousand Oaks, CA: Ontario Principals Council & Corwin Press.

Fullan, M. (2006). *Turnaround leadership.* San Francisco: Jossey Bass.

Fullan, M. (2009). Large scale education reform comes of age. *Journal of Educational Change,* 10(2-3), 101-113.

Fullan, M., & Miles, M. (1992). 'Getting reform right: What works and what doesn't'. *Phi Delta Kappan, 73*(10), 744 -752.

Gabriel, Y. (2000). *Storytelling in organisations. Facts, fictions and fantasies.* Oxford: Oxford University Press.

Gee, J., Hull, G., & Lankshear, C. (1996). *The new work order: Behind the language of the new capitalism.* Australia: Allen and Unwin.

Gewirtz, S. (2002). *The managerial school. Post-welfarism and social justice in education.* London: Routledge.

Gibbons, S., & Telhaj, S. (2006). *Peer effects and pupil attainment: evidence from secondary school transition.* London: Centre for the Economics of Education, London School of Economics.

Gillbourn, D., & Youdell, D. (2000). *Rationing education. Policy, practice, reform and equity.* Buckingham & Philadelphia: Open University Press.

Gitlin, A., & Margonis, F. (1995). 'The political aspect of reform: Teacher resistance is good sense'. *American Journal of Education,* 103 (4), 377-405.

Glickman, C. (2002). *Leadership for learning. How to help teachers succeed.* Alexandria, Virginia: Association for Supervision and Curriculum Development.

Godard, J. T. (2003). Leadership in the (Post) Modern era. In N. Bennett & L. Anderson (eds.), *Rethinking educational leadership. Challenging the conventions.* London: Sage.

Gonzales, N., Moll, L., & Amanti, C. (2005). *Funds of knowledge.* Mahwah, NJ: Lawrence Erlbaum.

Goodlad, J. (1994). *Educational renewal: better teachers, better schools.* San Francisco: Jossey Bass.

Goodman, D. (1979). *Educational disadvantage: A bibliography.* Canberra: Commonwealth Schools Commission, AGPS.

Goodman, J., Baron, D., & Myers, C. (2004). 'Constructing a democratic foundation for school-based reform'. In F. English (ed.), *The SAGE handbook of educational leadership. Advances in theory, research and practice* (pp. 297 - 331). Thousand Oaks CA: Sage.

Gorard, S., Taylor, C., & Fitz, J. (2003). *Schools, markets and choice policies.* London: RoutledgeFalmer.

Gordon, J., & Patterson, J. A. (2008). "It's what we've always been doing': Exploring tensions between school culture and change. *Journal of Educational Change*, 9(1), 17-35.

Grace, G. (1995). *School leadership. Beyond education management. An essay in policy scholarship.* London: Falmer Press.

Grainger, T., Gooch, K., & Lambirth, A. (2005). *Creativity and writing: Developing voice and verve in the classroom.* London: Routledge.

Gray, J. (2000). *Teachers at the center: A memoir of the early years of the National Writing Project.* Berkeley, CA: National Writing Project.

Griffith, A., & Smith, D. (2005). *Mothering for schooling.* New York: RoutledgeFalmer.

Gronn, P. (2003). *The new work of educational leaders: Changing leadership practice in an era of school reform.* London: Paul Chapman Publishing.

Gunter, H. (1997). *Rethinking education: The consequences of Jurassic management.* London & Herndon: Cassell.

Gunter, H. (2005). *Leading teachers.* London: Continuum.

Gurr, D. (1996). 'On conceptualising school leadership: time to abandon transformational leadership?' *Leading and Managing*, 2(3), 221-239.

Hall, G., & Hord, S. (1987). *Change in schools. Facilitating the process.* Albany, NY: State University of New York Press.

Hallgarten, J., & Edwards, L. (2000). *Parents as partners: Findings of a programme of consultation with Wednesbury parents. Wednesbury Education Action Zone.* London: Institute for Public Policy Research.

Hallgarten, J., & Watling, R. (2001). 'Buying power: the role of the private sector in Education Action Zones (1)'. *School Leadership and Management, 21*(2), 143-157.

Hargreaves, A. (1991). 'Contrived collegiality: the micropolitics of teacher collaboration'. In J. Blase (ed.), *The Politics of Life in Schools: Power, Conflict and Cooperation.* (pp. 46 - 72). Newbury Park, CA: Sage.

Hargreaves, A. (1994). *Changing teachers, changing times: Teachers' work and culture in the postmodern age.* London: Continuum.

Hargreaves, A. (2003). *Teaching in the knowledge society. Education in the age of insecurity.* Buckingham: Open University Press.

Hargreaves, A. (ed.). (1996). *Rethinking educational change with heart and mind.* Alexandria, VA: Association for Supervision and Curriculum Development.

Hargreaves, A., & Fink, D. (2006). *Sustainable leadership.* San Francisco, CA: Jossey Bass.

Hargreaves, A., & Goodson, I. (2006). 'Educational change over time? The sustainability and nonsustainability of three decades of secondary school change and continuity'. *Educational Administration Quarterly, 42*(1), 3-41.

Harris, A. (2000). 'Successful school improvement in the United Kingdom and Canada'. *Canadian Journal of Educational Administration*(15), **http://www.unmanitoba.ca/publications/cjeap/articles/harris.html.** Accessed 26 April, 2010

Harris, A. (2003). 'Teacher leadership as distributed leadership: heresy, fantasy or possibility?' *School Leadership and Management, 23*(3), 313-324.

Harris, A., & Chapman, C. (2002). *Effective leadership in schools facing challenging circumstances.* Nottingham: National College for School Leadership.

Harris, A., James, S., Gunraj, J., Clarke, P., & Harris, B. (2006). *Improving schools in exceptionally challenging circumstances: Tales from the frontline.* London: Continuum.

Harris, B., Vincent, K., Thomson, P., & Toalster, R. (2006). 'Does every child know they matter? Pupils' views of one alternative to exclusion'. *Pastoral Care in Education, 24*(2), 28-38.

Harrison, C., *et al* (2003). *ImpaCT2: The impact of information and communication technologies on pupil learning and attainment.* Coventry: BECTA.

Hart, S., Dixon, A., Drummond, M. J., & McIntyre, D. (2004). *Learning without limits.* Buckingham: Open University Press.

Hasci, T. (2002). *Children as pawns. The politics of education reform.* Cambridge, MA: Harvard University Press.

Hatcher, R. (2005). 'The distribution of leadership and power in schools'. *British Journal of Sociology of Education, 26*(2), 253–267.

Hatton, E., Munns, G., & Dent, J. N. (1996). 'Teaching children in poverty: Three Australian primary school responses'. *British Journal of Sociology of Education 17*(1) 39 - 52

Hayes, D., Mills, M., Christie, P., & Lingard, B. (2005). *Teachers and schooling: Making a difference: Productive pedagogies, assessment and performance.* Sydney: Allen & Unwin.

Holdsworth, R. (2000). 'Schools that create real roles of value for young people'. *Prospects, 115*(3), 349-362.

Holdsworth, R., Stafford, J., Stokes, H., & Tyler, D. (2001). *Student Action Teams - An evaluation: 1999-2000. Working Paper 21.* Melbourne: Australian Youth Research Centre.

Hollins, K., Gunter, H., & Thomson, P. (2006). 'Living improvement: a case study of a school in England'. *Improving Schools, 9*(2), 141-152.

Hopkins, D., Ainscow, M., & West, M. (1994). *School improvement in an era of change*. London: Cassell.

Hopkins, D., & Reynolds, D. (2001). 'The past, present and future of school improvement: towards the "third age"'. *British Educational Research Journal, 27*(4), 459-476.

Howley, C. (2003). *Small schools. ERIC Clearinghouse on Rural Education and Small Schools.*

Hughes, P., & MacNaughton, G. (2000). 'Consensus, dissensus or community: the politics of parent involvement in early childhood education'. *Contemporary Issues in Early Childhood, 1*(3), 241-158.

Jeffrey, B. (2006). *Creative learning practices: European experiences.* London: The Tufnell Press.

Jones, K., & Bird, K. (2000). '"Partnership" as strategy: public-private relations in Education Action Zones'. *British Educational Research Journal, 26*(4), 491-507.

Joyner, E., Comer, J. P., & Ben-Avie, M. (2004). *The field guide to Comer schools in action.* Thousand Oaks: Corwin.

Kamler, B., & Thomson, P. (2006). *Helping doctoral students write: Pedagogies for supervision.* London: Routledge.

Kemmis, S., Cole, P., & Suggett, D. (1983). *The socially critical school.* Melbourne: VISE.

Kemmis, S., & McTaggart, R. (eds.). (1988). *The Action Research Planner: Action Research and the Critical Analysis of Pedagogy* (3rd ed.). Geelong: Deakin University.

Kendall, L., O'Donnell, L., Golden, S., Ridley, K., Machin, S., Rutt, S., *et al* (2005). *Excellence in Cities. The national evaluation of a policy to raise standards in urban schools 2000-2003. Research Report 675B.* London: Department for Education and Skills.

Kenway, J., & Bullen, E. (2001). *Consuming children: Education, Entertainment and Advertising.* Buckingham: Open University Press.

Kenway, J., Bullen, E., & Robb, S. (2004). *Innovation and tradition. The arts, humanities and the knowledge economy.* New York: Peter Lang.

Keys, W., Sharp, C., Greene, K., & Grayson, H. (2003). *Successful leadership of schools in urban and challenging contexts.* Nottingham: National College for School Leadership.

Kincheloe, J. (1999). *How do we tell the workers? The socioeconomic foundations of work and vocational education.* Boulder, CO: Westview Press.

Kohn, A. (1998). *What to look for in classrooms and other essays.* San Francisco, CA: Jossey Bass.

Kress, G., Jewitt, C., Bourne, J., Franks, A., Hardcastle, J., Jones, K., Reid, E. (2005). *English in urban classrooms. A multimodal perspective on teaching and learning.* London: RoutledgeFalmer.

Kugelmass, J. (2004). *The inclusive school. Sustaining equity and standards.* New York: Teachers College Press.

Ladwig, J., Currie, J., & Chadbourne, R. (1994). *Toward rethinking Australian schools: A synthesis of the reported practices of the National Schools Project.* Ryde, New South Wales: National Schools Network.

Lambert, L. (1998). *Building leadership capacity in schools.* Alexandria, VA: Association for Supervision and Curriculum Development.

Lankshear, C., Bigum, C., Durrant, C., Green, B., Murray, J., Morgan, W., *et al* (1997). *Digital rhetorics. Literacies and technologies in education - Current practices and future directions. Volumes 1-3.* Canberra: Department of Employment, Education, Training, and Youth Affairs

Leithwood, K., Aitken, R., & Jantzi, D. (2006). *Making schools smarter: Leading with evidence.* Thousand Oaks: Corwin Press.

Leithwood, K., & Jantzi, D. (1999). 'The relative effects of principal and teacher sources of leadership on student engagement with school'. *Educational Administration Quarterly, 35* (Supplemental, December), 679-706.

Leithwood, K., & Reihl, C. (2003). *What we know about successful school leadership.* Philadelphia, PA: Laboratory for Student Success, Temple University.

Leithwood, K., Steinbach, R., & Jantzi, D. (2002). 'School leadership and teachers' motivation to implement accountability policies'. *Educational Administration Quarterly, 38*(1), 94-119.

Levin, B. (2001). *Reforming education: From origins to outcomes.* London: Falmer Press.

Levin, B. (2008). *How to change 500 schools. A practical and positive approach for leading change at every level.* Cambridge, MA: Harvard Education Press.

Levin, B., & Riffel, J. A. (1997). *Schools and the changing world. Struggling toward the future.* London, Washington DC: Falmer Press.

Lewin, C., Mavers, D., & Somekh, B. (2003). 'Broadening access to the curriculum through using technology to link home and school: A critical analysis of reforms intended to improve students' educational attainment'. *The Curriculum Journal, 14*(1), 23-53.

Lieberman, A., & Grolnick, M. (1996). 'Networks and reform in American education'. *Teachers College Record, 98*(1), 7-46.

Lieberman, A., & McLaughlin, M. W. (1992). 'Networks for educational change: Powerful and problematic'. *Phi Delta Kappan, 73*(9), 673-677.

Lieberman, A., & Wood, D. (2003). *Inside the National Writing Project: Connecting learning and classroom teaching.* New York: Teachers College Press.

Lindsay, G., Pather, S., & Strand, S. (2006). *Special educational needs and ethnicity: issues of over and under representation. Research Report RR757.* London: Department for Education and Skills.

Lingard, B. (1998). 'The Disadvantaged Schools Program: caught between literacy and local management of schools'. *International Journal of Inclusive Education, 2*(1), 1-14.

Lingard, B., Christie, P., Hayes, D., & Mills, M. (2003). *Leading learning: Making hope practical in schools.* Buckingham: Open University Press.

Lipman, P. (1998). *Race, class, and power in school restructuring.* New York: State University of New York Press.

Livingstone, D. (1998). *The education-jobs gap: Underemployment or economic democracy.* Boulder, CO: Westview Press.

Lodge, C., & Reed, J. (2003). 'Transforming school improvement now and for the future'. *Journal of Educational Change, 4* (1), 45-62.

Louis, K. S., & Miles, M. (1990). *Improving the urban high school. What works and why.* New York: Teachers College Press.

Lupton, R. (2003). *Poverty street: The dynamics of neighbourhood decline and renewal (Case studies on poverty, place and policy).* Bristol, UK: The Policy Press.

Lupton, R. (2004). *Schools in disadvantaged areas: Recognising context and raising performance. CASE paper 76.* London: Centre for Analysis of Social Exclusion, London School of Economics.

Lyman, L., & Villani, C. (2004). *Best leadership practices for high-poverty schools.* Lanham, MD: Scarecrow.

Macbeath, J. (1999). *Schools should speak for themselves.* London: Falmer.

Macbeath, J., Demetriou, H., Rudduck, J., & Myers, K. (2003). *Consulting pupils: A toolkit for teachers.* Cambridge: Pearson Publishing.

Macbeath, J., Jakobsen, L., Meuret, D., & Schratz, M. (2000). *Self evaluation in European schools: A story of change.* London: Routledge.

MacBeath, J., & Sugimine, H. (2003). *Self evaluation in the global classroom.* London: Routledge.

MacDonald, B., & Walker, R. (1976). *Changing the curriculum.* London: Open Books.

MacGilchrist, B., Reed, J., & Myers, K. (2004). *The intelligent school (2nd edition).* London: Sage Publications.

Machin, S., Telhaj, S., & Wilson, J. (2006). *The mobility of English school children.* London: Centre for the Economics of Education, London School of Economics.

Maclure, M., & Walker, B. (2000). 'Disenchanted evenings: the social organisation of talk in parents-teacher consultation in UK secondary schools'. *British Journal of Sociology of Education, 21*(1), 5-21.5

Makin, L., & Spedding, S. (2003). '"Cause they trust their parents, don't they?" : Supporting literacy in the first three years of life'. *Australian Research in Early Childhood Education, 10*(2), 39-49.

Matthews, H., & Limb, H. (2003). 'Another white elephant? Youth councils as democratic structures'. *Space and Polity, 7*(2), 173-192.

Maxcy, S. (1995). *Democracy, chaos, and new school order.* Thousand Oaks, CA: Corwin Press.

McKinley, S., & Else, A. (2002). *Maori parents and education.* Wellington: New Zealand Council for Educational Research.

McLaughlin, C., Black-Hawkins, K., Brindley, S., McIntyre, D., & Taber, K. (2006). *Researching schools: Stories from a schools-university partnership for educational research.* London: Routledge.

McLaughlin, M. W., & Talbert, J. E. (2001). *Professional communities and the work of high school teaching.* Chicago: University of Chicago Press.

McRae, D. (1990). *Getting it right: schools serving disadvantaged communities. Commissioned Report 2.* Canberra: Schools Council, National Board of Employment, Education and Training.

Meier, D. (1995). *The power of their ideas: Lessons for America from a small school in Harlem.* Boston: Beacon Press.

Middlewood, D., Parker, R., & Beere, J. (2005). *Creating a learning school.* London: Paul Chapman.

Miron, L., & Lauria, M. (2005). *Urban schools: The new social spaces of resistance.* New York: Peter Lang.

Moll, L., Tapia, J., & Whitmore, K. (1993). 'Living knowledge: the social distribution of cultural resources for thinking'. In G. Salomon (ed.), *Distributed cognitions* (pp. 139-163). Cambridge: Cambridge University Press.

Moos, L., & Macbeath, J. (2004). *Democratic learning: the challenge to school effectiveness.* London: RoutledgeFalmer.

Mulford, B. (2003). *School leaders: changing roles and impact on teacher and school effectiveness.* OECD: Paris.

Mulkeen, A. (2003). 'What can policy makers do to encourage integration of information and communications technology? Evidence from the Irish school system'. *Technology, Pedagogy and Education, 12*(2), 277-293.

Muncey, D. E., & Macquillan, P. J. (1996). *Reform and resistance in schools and classrooms. An ethnographic view of the Coalition of Essential Schools.* New Haven CT: Yale University Press.

Mundy, K. (2005). Globalization and Educational Change: New Policy Worlds. In N. Bascia, A. Cumming, A. Datnow, K. Leithwood & D. Livingstone (eds.), *International handbook of educational policy* (pp. 3-17). Dordrecht: Springer.

National Statistics. (2006). *Statistics of education: Trends in attainment gaps: 2005.* London: National Statistics.

Newmann, F., & Associates. (1996). *Authentic achievement: Restructuring schools for intellectual quality.* San Francisco: Jossey Bass.

Noblit, G., Dickson, C., H, Wilson, B. A., & McKinney, M. B. (2009). *Creating and sustaining arts-based school reform. The A+ schools program.* New York: Routledge.

Oakes, J., Wells, A. S., Jones, M., & Datnow, A. (1997). 'Detracking: The social construction of ability, cultural politics, and resistance to reform'. *Teachers College Record, 98*(3), 482 - 510.

Oden, S., Schweinhart, L., Weikart, D., Marcus, S., & Xie, Y. (2000). *Into adulthood: A study of the effects of Head Start:* Ypsilanti, MI: High/Scope Press.

OECD. (2002). *Schooling for tomorrow: OECD scenarios.* Nottingham: National College for School Leadership.
http://www.oecd.org/document/33/0,3343,en_2649_35845581_38981601_1_1_1_1,00.html Accessed 26 April, 2010

OECD. (2006). *Think scenarios, rethink education.* Paris: Centre for Educational Research and Innovation, OECD.

OECD. (undated). *CERI -The OECD schooling scenarios in brief.*
http://www.oecd.org/document/10/0,2340,en_2649_34521_2078922_1_1_1_37455,00.html. Accessed 26 April, 2010.

OfSTED. (2002). *The curriculum in successful primary schools.* London: Office for Standards in Education.

O'Hair, M. J., & Veugelers, W. (2005). 'The case for network learning'. In W. Veugelers & M. J. O'Hair (eds.), *Network learning for organisational change* (pp. 1-16). Buckingham: Open University Press.

Pacione, M. (Ed.). (1997). *Britain's cities: Geographies of division in urban Britain.* London: Routledge.

Papert, S. (1993). *The children's machine: Rethinking school in the age of the computer.* New York: Basic Books.

Pennell, J., & Firestone, R. (1996). 'Changing classroom practices through teacher networks: Matching program features with teacher characteristics and circumstances'. *Teachers College Record, 98*(1), 46-76.

Pounder, D. (1998). *Restructuring schools for collaboration. Promises and pitfalls.* New York: State University of New York.

Powell, A., Farrar, E., & Cohen, D. (1985). *The shopping mall high school: Winners and losers in the educational marketplace.* Boston: Houghton Miflin.

Putnam, R. (1995). 'Bowling alone: America's declining social capital'. *Journal of Democracy, 6*(1), 65-78.

Raywid, M. (1993). 'Finding time for collaboration'. *Educational Leadership, 51*(1), 30-34.

Reay, D. (1998). *Class work: Mothers' involvement in their children's primary schooling.* London: University College Press.

Reich, R. (1991). *The work of nations. A blueprint for the future.* New York: Simon and Schuster.

Reid, K. (2002). 'Mentoring with disaffected pupils'. *Mentoring and Tutoring, 10*(2), 153-169.

Riddell, R. (2003). *Schools for our cities: Urban learning in the 21st century.* Stoke on Trent: Trentham.

Rifkin, J. (1995). *The end of work: The decline of the global labour force and the dawn of the post market era.* New York: Putnam.

Rust, F. O. C., & Freidus, H. (eds.). (2001). *Guiding school change: The role and work of change agents.* New York: Teachers College Press.

Rutter, M., Mortimore, P., & Maugham, B. (1979). *Fifteen thousand hours: Secondary schools and their effects on children.* Boston: Harvard University Press.

Ryan, J. (1998). 'Critical leadership for education in a postmodern world: Emancipation, resistance and communal action'. *International Journal of Leadership in Education, 1*(3), 257-278.

Ryan, J. (2000). 'Educative leadership for culturally diverse schools'. *Leading and Managing, 6*(1), 1-20.

Ryan, J. (2003). *Leading diverse schools. (Studies in Educational Leadership).* Dordrecht: Kluwer.

Ryan, J. (2005). *Inclusive leadership.* San Francisco: Jossey Bass.

Schon, D. (1987). *Educating the reflective practitioner: toward a new design for teaching and learning in the professions.* New York: Basic Books.

Schon, D. (ed.). (1991). *The reflective turn: Case studies in and on Educational Practice.* New York: Teachers College Press.

School of Education University of Queensland. (2001). *Queensland School Reform Longitudinal Study (QSLRS).* Brisbane: Department of Education, Queensland.

Sefton Green, J. (ed.). (1998). *Digital diversions: Youth culture in the age of multimedia.* London: UCL Press.

Seller, W., & Hannay, L. (2000). 'Inside-outside change facilitation: structural and cultural considerations'. In N. Bascia & A. Hargreaves (eds.), *The sharp edge of education change: Teaching, leading and the realities of reform* (pp. 197-216). London: RoutledgeFalmer.

Senge, P. (1990). *The Fifth discipline: The art and practice of the learning organisation.* New York: Doubleday.

Senge, P., Cambron-McCabe, N., Lucas, T., Smith, B., Dutton, J., & Kleiner, A. (2000). *Schools that learn: A Fifth Discipline fieldbook for educators, parents, and everyone who cares about education.* New York & London: Currency, Doubleday.

Sennett, R. (1998). *The corrosion of character. The personal consequences of work in the new capitalism.* New York: W.W. Norton & Company.

Sharratt, L., & Fullan, M. (2009). *Realization: the change imperative for deepening district-wide reform.* SAGE Publications.

Shields, C. (2003). *Good intentions are not enough. Transformative leadership for communities of difference.* Lanham, MD: Scarecrow Press.

Shields, C., Bishop, R., & Mazawi, A. E. (2005). *Pathologising practices. The impact of deficit thinking on education.* New York: Peter Lang.

Shields, C., & Edwards, M. (2005). *Dialogue is not just talk: A new ground for educational leadership.* New York: Peter Lang.

Shumow, L., & Miller, J. (2001). 'Parents' at-home involvement and at-school academic involvement with young adolescents'. *Journal of Early Adolescence, 21*(1), 68-91.

Silins, H., & Mulford, B. (2004). 'Schools as learning organisations – Effects on teacher leadership and student outcomes'. *School Effectiveness and School Improvement, 15*(3-4), 443–466.

Simpson, D. (2001). The impact of breakfast clubs on pupil attendance and punctuality. *Research in Education, 66*, 76-83.

Simpson, D., & Cieslik, M. (2000). 'Expanding study support nationally: implications from an evaluation of the East Middlesborough Education Action Zone's programme'. *Educational Studies, 26*(4), 503-515.

Sizer, T. (1985). *Horace's compromise. The dilemma of the American high school.* Boston: Houghton Miflin.

Sizer, T. (1992). *Horace's school. Redesigning the American high school.* Boston: Houghton Miflin.

Sizer, T. (1996). *Horace's hope. What works for the American high school.* Boston: Houghton Miflin.

Slee, R., Weiner, G., & Tomlinson, S. (eds.). (1998). *School effectiveness for whom? Challenges to the school effectiveness and school improvement movements.* London: Falmer.

Smith, A., & Wohlstetter, P. (2001). 'Reform through school networks: a new kind of authority and accountability'. *Educational Policy, 15*(4), 499-519.

Smith, P., Molnar, A., & Zahorik, J. (2005). *Class-size reduction: a fresh look at the data.* University of Wisconsin-Milwaukee & Arizona State University: **http://epicpolicy.org/publication/class-size-reduction-a-fresh-look-data** Accessed 26 April, 2010

Smyth, J. (ed.). (1993). *A socially critical view of the self managing school.* London: Falmer Press.

Smyth, J., & Hattam, R. (2004). *Dropping out, drifting off, being excluded: becoming somebody without school.* New York: Peter Lang.

Somekh, B. (2000). 'Changing conceptions of action research'. In H. Altrichter & J. Elliott (eds.), *Images of educational change* (pp. 111 - 122). Buckingham: Open University Press.

Southworth, G., & Coles, M. (eds.). (2005). *Developing leadership. Creating the schools of the future.* Buckingham: Open University Press.

Spender, D. (1995). *Nattering on the net. Women, power and cyberspace.* Melbourne: Spinifex.

Spillane, J. (2006). *Distributed leadership.* San Francisco: Jossey Bass.

Starratt, R. (2003). *Centering educational administration: Cultivating meaning, community, responsibility.* Mahwah, New Jersey: Lawrence Erlbaum

Stenhouse, L. (1975). *An introduction to curriculum research and development.* London: Heinemann.

Stoll, L., Earl, L., & Fink, D. (2003). *It's about learning (and it's about time): What's in it for schools?* London: RoutledgeFalmer.

Stoll, L., & Fink, D. (1996). *Changing our schools: linking school effectiveness and school improvement.* Buckingham: Open University Press.

Stoll, L., & Myers, K. (eds.). (1998). *No quick fixes: Perspectives on schools in difficulty.* London: Falmer.

Strachan, J. (1998). 'Feminist leadership: leading for social justice'. *Waikato Journal of Education, 4*, 27-34.

Strahan, D., Cooper, J., & Ward, M. (2001). 'Middle school reform through data and dialogue: collaborative evaluation with 17 leadership teams'. *Evaluation Review, 25*(1), 72-99.

Stromquist, N., & Monkman, K. (eds.). (2000). *Globalisation and education: Integration and contestation across cultures.* Lanham, MD: Rowman & Littlefield.

Stubbs, M. (2003). *Ahead of the class: How an inspiring headmistress gave children back their future.* London: John Murray.

Tatto, M. T., et al (2001). 'The challenges and tensions in reconstructing teacher-parents relations in the context of reform: a case study'. *Teachers and Teaching: Theory and Practice, 7*(3), 315-333.

Taylor, F. W. (1911/1947). *Scientific management.* New York: Harper & Brothers.

Teddlie, C., & Reynolds, D. (eds.). (2000). *The international handbook of school effectiveness.* London: Falmer.

The New London Group. (1996). 'A pedagogy of multiliteracies: designing social futures'. *Harvard Educational Review, 66*(1), 363 - 376.

Thomson, P. (1993). School change. Critical pedagogy in action. *Education Links, 43*, 25 -29.

Thomson, P. (1994). *Local decision making and management.* Adelaide: Joint Principals Associations, South Australia.

Thomson, P. (1998). *The changing role of the principal* (CD -Rom). Adelaide: South Australian Secondary Principals Association.

Thomson, P. (1999a). 'Against the odds: developing school programs that make a difference for students and families in communities placed "at risk"'. *Childrenz Issues, 3*(1), 7-13.

Thomson, P. (1999b). *Doing justice: stories of everyday life in disadvantaged schools and neighbourhoods.* Unpublished PhD, Deakin University. Accessible via the Australian Digital Thesis programme., Geelong.

Thomson, P. (2000). 'Like schools, educational disadvantage and "thisness"'. *Australian Educational Researcher, 27*(3), 151-166.

Thomson, P. (2002). *Schooling the rustbelt kid: Making the difference in changing times.* Sydney: Allen & Unwin (Trentham Books UK).

Thomson, P. (2007). 'Making education more equitable: What can policymakers learn from the Australian Disadvantaged Schools Programme?' In R. Teese, S., Lamb, M. Duru-Bellat & S. Helme., (eds.), *International Studies in Educational Inequality, Theory and Policy.* Springer, Netherlands

Thomson, P. (2007). 'Leading schools in high poverty neighbourhoods: The National College for School Leadership and beyond.' In W. Pink & W. Noblit (eds.), *International handbook of urban education* (pp. 1049-1078). Springer Netherlands

Thomson, P., & Blackmore, J. (2006). 'Beyond the power of one: redesigning the work of school principals and schools'. *Journal of Educational Change. 7*(3): 161-177.

Thomson, P., Harris, B., Vincent, K., & Toalster, R. (2005). *Evaluation of the Coalfields Alternatives To Exclusion (CATE) programme.* Nottingham: Centre for Research in Equity and Diversity in Education, School of Education, The University of Nottingham.

Thomson, P., McQuade, V., & Rochford, K. (2005). "My little special house": re-forming the risky geographies of middle school girls at Clifftop College. In G. Lloyd (ed.), *Problem girls. Understanding and supporting troubled and troublesome girls and young women* (pp. 172 - 189). London: RoutledgeFalmer.

Thomson, P., & Sanders, E. (2009). Creativity and whole school change: an investigation of English headteachers' practices. *Journal of Educational Change, preprint online.*

Thomson, P., & Wilkins, P. (1997). *Survey of spending in DSP schools.* Adelaide: Joint Principals Associations, South Australia.

Thrupp, M. (1999). *Schools making a difference: let's be realistic! School mix, school effectiveness and the social limits of reform.* Buckingham, Philadelphia: Open University Press.

Thrupp, M. (2006). *School improvement. An unofficial approach.* London: Continuum.

Thrupp, M., & Wilmott, R. (2003). *Educational management in managerialist times: beyond the textual apologists.* Buckingham: Open University Press.

Tittle, D. (1995). *Welcome to Heights High. The crippling politics of restructuring America's public schools.* Columbus: Ohio State University Press.

Tooley, J. (2000). *Reclaiming education.* London & New York: Cassell.

Toynbee, P. (2003). *Hard work: Life in low-pay Britain.* London: Bloomsbury.

Troman, G., & Woods, P. (2000). 'Careers under stress: teacher adaptations at a time of intensive reform'. *Journal of Educational Change, 1*(3), 253-275.

Tubin, D., Mioduser, D., Nachmais, R., & Forkosh-Barush, A. (2003). 'Domains and levels of pedagogical innovation in schools using ICT: ten schools in Israel'. *Education and Information Technologies, 8*(2), 127-145.

Tyack, D., & Cuban, L. (1995). *Tinkering toward utopia. A century of public school reform.* San Francisco: Jossey Bass.

Tyack, D., & Tobin, W. (1994). 'The grammar of schooling: why has it been so hard to change?' *American Educational Research Journal, 31*(3), 453-480.

Valencia, R. (ed.). (1997). *The evolution of deficit thinking. Educational thought and practice.* London: Falmer.

Vincent, C. (1993). 'Community participation? The establishment of 'City's Parents' Centre'. *British Educational Research Journal, 19*(3), 227-242.

Vincent, C. (1996). 'Parent empowerment? Collective action and inaction in education'. *Oxford Review of Education, 22*(4), 465-483.

Vincent, C. (2000). *Including parents? Education, citizenship and parental agency.* Buckingham: Open University Press.

Vulliamy, G., & Webb, R. (2006). *Coming full circle? The impact of New Labour's education policies on primary school teachers' work.* London: Association of Teachers and Lecturers.

Wang, M. C., Haertel, G. D., and Walberg, H. J. 1998. *Achieving student success: A handbook of widely implemented research-based educational reform models.* Philadelphia, PA: Temple University Center for Research in Human Development and Education

Walker, M., & Unterhalter, E. (eds.). (2007). *Amartya Sen's capability approach and social justice in education.* New York: Palgrave.

Warren Little, J. (1993). 'Teachers' professional development in a climate of educational reform'. *Educational Evaluation and Policy Analysis, 15* (2), pp. 129-151.

Warren Little, J. (1995). 'Contested ground. The basis of teacher leadership in two restructuring high schools'. *Elementary School Journal, 96*(1), 47-63.

Warren Little, J. (1996). 'The emotional contours and career trajectories of (disappointed) reform enthusiasts'. *Cambridge Journal of Education, 26*(3), 345-359.

Wasley, P. (1994). *Stirring the chalk dust: Tales of teachers changing classroom practice.* New York: Teachers College Press.

Wasley, P., Hampel, R., & Clark, R. (1997). *Kids and school reform.* San Francisco: Jossey Bass.

Waterman, R. (1993). *Adhocracy.* New York: W W Norton & Co.

Webber, R., & Butler, T. (2005). *Classifying pupils by where they live: how well does this predict variations in their GCSE results? CASA working paper 99.* London: Centre for Advanced Spatial Analysis. University College London, **http://www.casa.ucl.ac.uk/working_papers/paper99.pdf** Accessed 26 April, 2010

Weis, L., & Fine, M. (2001). 'Extraordinary conversations in public schools'. *Qualitative Studies in Education, 14*(4), 497-523.

Wenger, E. (1998). *Communities of practice. Learning, meaning and identity.* Cambridge: Cambridge University Press.

West, M., Ainscow, M., & Stanford, J. (2006). 'Achieving sustainable improvements in urban schools'. In M. Ainscow & M. West (eds.), *Improving urban schools. Leadership and collaboration* (pp. 46-57). Buckingham: Open University Press.

West-Burnham, J. (2005). 'Leadership for personalisation'. In J. West-Burnham & M. Coates (eds.), *Personalised learning: Transforming education for every child* (pp. 98-114). Stafford: Network Educational Press.

Westheimer, J. (1998). *Among schoolteachers: Community, autonomy and ideology in teachers' work.* New York: Teachers College Press.

Wexler, P., Crichlow, W., Kern, J., & Martusewicz, R. (1992). *Becoming somebody. Toward a social psychology of school.* London: Falmer Press.

White, R. C. (2000). *The school of tomorrow: Values and vision.* Buckingham: Open University Press.

Whitty, G., Power, S., & Halpin, D. (1998). *Devolution and choice in education: the school, the state and the market.* Buckingham: Open University Press.

Wigman, B. (1997). 'Competency-based training - Taylorism revisited?' In C. O'Farrell (ed.), *Foucault. The legacy* (pp. 614 - 619). Brisbane: QUT Press.

Willis, P. (1977). *Learning to labour. How working class kids get working class jobs.* London: Saxon House.

Wilson, B., & Corbett, H. D. (2001). *Listening to urban kids: School reform and the teachers they want.* New York: State University of New York Press.

Wilson, S. M. (2003). *California dreaming: Reforming mathematics education.* New Haven CT: Yale University Press.

Winkley, D. (2002). *Handsworth revolution: The odyssey of a school.* London: Giles De La Mare.

Winter, R. (1989). *Learning from experience: Principles and practice in action research.* Lewes: Falmer Press.

Wohlstetter, P., Van Kirk, A., Robertson, P., & Mohrman, S. (1997). *Organising for successful school-based management.* Virginia: Association for Supervision and Curriculum Development.

Woods, P. (2005). *Democratic leadership in education.* London: Paul Chapman.

Woods, P., & Jeffrey, B. (1996). *Teachable moments. The art of teaching in primary schools.* Buckingham: Open University Press.

Woods, P., Jeffrey, B., Troman, G., & Boyle, M. (1997). *Restructuring schools, reconstructing teachers.* Buckingham: Open University Press.

Woods, P., & O'Shannessy, J. (2002). 'Reintroducing creativity: Day 10 at Hackelton school'. *The Curriculum Journal, 13*(2), 163-182.

Wrigley, T. (2003). *Schools of hope: a new agenda for school improvement.* Stoke on Trent: Trentham Books.

Wylie, C. (1997). *Self-managing schools: seven years on - what have we learnt?* Auckland: New Zealand Council for Educational Research.

York-Barr, J., & Duke, K. (2004). 'What do we know about teacher leadership? Findings from two decades of scholarship'. *Review of Educational Research, 74*(3), 255-316.

Young, M. (1998). *The curriculum of the future: from the 'new sociology of education' to a critical theory of learning.* London: RoutledgeFalmer.

Zill, N., Resnick, G., Kim, K., O'Donnell, K., Sorongon, A., Hubbell McKey, R., *et al* (2003). *Head Start FACES 2000: A whole-child perspective on program performance.* Washington, DC: Child Outcomes Research and Evaluation **http://www.acf.hhs.gov/programs/opre/hs/faces/reports/faces00_4thprogress/faces00_4thprogress.pdf.** Accessed 26 April, 2010